GET RICH
with
twitter

GET RICH with twitter

Harness the Power of the
Twitterverse and
Reach More Customers
than Ever Before

DENNIS L. PRINCE

Mc
Graw
Hill

New York Chicago San Francisco Lisbon London Madrid Mexico City
Milan New Delhi San Juan Seoul Singapore Sydney Toronto

Library of Congress Cataloging-in-Publication Data

Prince, Dennis L.
  Get rich with Twitter / by Dennis L. Prince. — 1st ed.
    p.   cm.
  Includes index.
  ISBN-13: 978-0-07-163844-9
  ISBN-10: 0-07-163844-X
    1. Twitter.   2. Internet marketing.   3. Business communication.   4. Online social
networks.   I. Title.

  HF5415.1265.P75   2010
  658.8'72—dc22   2010000280

1 2 3 4 5 6 7 8 9 10 11 12 13 14 15   DOC/DOC   1 9 8 7 6 5 4 3 2 1 0

ISBN   978-0-07-163844-9
MHID   0-07-163844-X

McGraw-Hill books are available at special quantity discounts to use as premiums and sales promotions or for use in corporate training programs. To contact a representative, please e-mail us at bulksales@mcgraw-hill.com.

While the author and publisher have done their best to ensure that the Twitter screen shots appearing in this book are current at the time of printing, the reader must be aware that due to the ever-evolving technology of the medium it is impossible to guarantee the accuracy of every single screen shot once the book has been published.

Readers should know that online businesses have risk. Readers who participate in marketing and selling online do so at their own risk. The author and publisher of this book cannot guarantee financial success and therefore disclaim any liability, loss, or risk sustained, either directly or indirectly, as a result of using the information given in this book.

Contents

GET RICH
with
twitter

Introduction

IF YOU WERE TO answer the question "What are you doing?" or "What's happening?" at this very moment, you'd likely say you were reading the introduction to a book. Maybe you are looking through this book as you wait outside the venue for some key event to begin. Perhaps, as you read the first few sentences of this book, you glance over your shoulder only to realize that you are standing alongside a very interesting person—a person of influence or a celebrity. You can't help but think to yourself, "Wow! I bet so-and-so would *love* to know that I'm standing right next to this person!" Now, I know that not every second of your life is as heart-pumping and share-worthy as the moment you realize that you're literally rubbing elbows with, say, Donald Trump. But whatever it is that you're doing right now, you'd likely find that someone, somewhere, is curious to hear about it; so, let it be known.

This is the core concept behind Twitter, the social networking platform that gives everyday people the ability to broadcast to others what they are doing and what's happening *as it actually occurs*. It's the most elemental form of message dispersal, whether you call it "mass communication," "real-time notification," or "getting the word out." Simply put, Twitter allows its users to construct and transmit short, informative bursts, called "tweets," of just 140 or fewer typewritten characters from a central hub, http://www.twitter.com, to a group of followers who have indicated their curiosity to learn about what a particular Twitter user is doing or thinking about. It's messaging that's short, sweet, and to the point.

Known as *microblogging*, tweeting via Twitter encourages communication of the most concise style in the form of information that can be quickly disseminated and digested for both sending and receiving sides. Microblog messages are designed to be transmitted and received via multiple methods, be it with a computer or within the tiny confines of a cell phone or PDA (personal digital assistant). Information that's broadcast in this fashion is of a style that aligns more with the thinking patterns of people in this new millennium in that it is fast-paced, to the point, and very targeted to those who really want to know. For consumers, this is the overdue antidote to the yadda-yadda-yadda syndrome that is manifested in unwanted e-mails and long-winded proclamations about products and services that, surely, you simply can't live without. And while it might seem initially counterintuitive, this sort of short and sweet communication is, for businesses and the people who run them, a prayer finally answered.

It all began with the simple question "What are you doing?" (evolving to the more encompassing "What's happening?"). The answer, however, brings up more questions for those who might consider responding to the inquiry. For example:

- If the key to "tweeting" is concise messaging, what is concise enough (and what might be too concise)?
- Does effective messaging include any specific style or tone to reach an audience?
- What exactly should a business say to others about what's happening (and what shouldn't be said)?
- How often should a business be tweeting to exert the most impact on both its sales and its audience?
- And how do you ensure effort poured into Twitter communication isn't quickly overlooked or forgotten? What if this is just some technological "fad"?

If these new questions seem daunting or dissuade you from thinking that adopting Twitter is good for you and your business, rest assured you are in good company. Others have voiced the same questions, and many have overcome these "barriers" and have developed a solid Twitter methodology and approach. If you're ready to step up to cutting-edge marketing through microblogging, you've come to the right place. In your hands is the guide that can help you make the most of Twitter and get the best result for your efforts as it pertains to your personal needs or business goals. And to think you have as valuable a tool as Twitter at your disposal all because you sensed the value in answering the questions "What are you doing?" and "What's happening?"

■ ■ ■ Personalized Marketing via Mass Communication

In this new age of doing business, it's arguable that "traditional" communication methods of decades past are on the path to obsolescence. Printed newspaper circulation is waning, while wastebaskets (and landfills) are fast becoming overrun with discarded direct mail materials. To the businessperson, this could be the undoing of establishing customer reach. However, thanks to the Internet and to Twitter specifically, that reach just became even easier, cheaper, and more engaging than ever before.

The value of Twitter in the hyper-evolving global market is that it takes an about-face approach to being heard among the din of other businesses' appeals and advances. No longer is it effective or even wise to oversaturate customers with advertisements. In fact, customers are actively seeking ways to avoid blaring announcements, interruptive online pitches, and virtual mountains of unwanted e-mail come-ons. Consumers have been clear about their frustration with these sorts of annoying and intrusive marketing methods. Instead, people are looking for those things that truly "speak" to them, their interests, and their own personal ideals. But the secret of making such personal contact with your customers doesn't, in most cases, come through personalized messages and styles adapted to varying customer tastes. Rather, Twitter succeeds where other marketing methodologies fail because by design it understands that consumers today feel most inclined toward products and services that *they themselves* seek out, not the other way around.

With Twitter, individuals and businesses are developing a message feed that their customers elect to *subscribe to*. When customers have this level of control over what they'll hear and what they'll tune out, you have the opportunity to say to them what they're truly interested in hearing.

■ ■ ■ Quick Messaging for Long-Term Loyalty

If you think Twitter is just another teen-angled social distraction, think again. While Twitter certainly serves the preadult crowd just looking to chat back and forth, businesses have adapted and honed the functionality as a new way to deliver their products to consumers in a focused manner. If the business's message is effective, the recipient of the message will instantly understand the product, its source, and where to acquire or learn more about it. In a textual flash, the consumer is given immediately usable information and can act upon it just as quickly. And in today's heavily informational culture, fast messaging that provides fast information is what enables businesses to communicate quickly and concisely to their audience of followers.

What businesses? News agencies such as CNN, BBC, Fox News, and others maintain active Twitter feeds to their "followers" (that's Twitter-talk for subscribers). Online media information and review sites such as DVD Verdict, Atlanta Music Guide, and GameSpy are Twitter-enabled. Home Depot established a Twitter presence in 2008 at the time of Hurricane Gustav, offering citizens up-to-the-minute tips and necessary supplies for proper hurricane preparedness.

You get the idea: establishing the type of market exposure that Twitter provides businesses could cost you a fortune and take years to accomplish by traditional means. But with Twitter, you can promote yourself and your business rapidly and routinely in a matter of only days.

Of course, because your followers can respond to your tweets within your Twitter home page, you will gain immediate feedback on your message effectiveness while getting to know who's following you.

■ ■ ■ What You'll Find in This Book

Given that the Internet and media outlets are abuzz with who's tweeting what, I will wager that you have heard of Twitter, and I will also bet you can imagine how ripe the Twitterverse is for your use. If you're not sure how to harness this quick yet constant buzz, this book has what you need to start tweeting, for fun and for profit. Here's a quick look at what you'll find within these pages.

■ ■ PART 1 UNDERSTANDING TWITTER

Twitter is relatively new, and, as such, this book presumes that you're venturing into the realm of Twitter as a bona fide newcomer (or "newbie"). Welcome! As said, you're in good company, and you're one of many who are motivated to harness this newest outreach opportunity. The first part of this book teaches you about the background of Twitter: who created it, why it's working, and who's using it. You'll learn about being a Twitter "friend" and how to build a loyal audience of "followers" who are eager to keep pace with your day-to-day activities (that is, you and *your business*). Most important, you'll discover how to use Twitter in a way that benefits your business yet doesn't require a wholesale exploitation of your "listeners." There's a fine balance to strike between messaging and marketing; if you're too heavy on one side or the other, your tweets will fall upon deaf ears. In this part of the book, you'll learn what it takes to establish solid footing within the Twitterverse.

■ ■ Part 2 Establishing and Tweaking Your Twitter Presence

If you think getting yourself established within the Twitterverse is cumbersome and labor-intensive, it's not. As a matter of fact, you can establish your own Twitter presence in mere minutes. Of course, there's a bit more to do after that, as you will need to customize and clarify your Twitter presence, but it's no arduous task. Within this section, you'll learn how to get started and get smoothly engaged with Twitter, and in no time at all, you will start looking as if you're a seasoned Twitter pro.

■ ■ Part 3 Advancing the Twitter Touch

This section provides an overview of logical next steps to take in order to get the most from your messaging—and that means further mining your Twitter experience to boost your presence and profits. From keeping your Twitter home page fresh and fun to discovering new ways to build your base of followers while keeping your current audience eager and attentive to your next tweet, this section gives you hints and suggestions for finding and tapping into additional messaging opportunities by marrying the emerging technology of Twitter to the time-tested tenets of marketing and effective communication.

■ ■ Part 4 Look, Listen, and Learn: Twitter Success Stories

In these days of nanosecond communication, it's understandable that we've become impatient when it comes to organically growing a successful endeavor. While you're certainly encouraged to experiment with your Twitter presence, tweaking it so that it truly reflects your persona and that of your business, it still makes good sense to study what other successful Twitter users are doing. Therefore, to wrap up your induction into the world of Twitter and tweeting, this part of the book focuses on eight compelling case studies of companies and organizations that have turned to Twitter to engage friends and customers in a fresh and results-oriented manner. These are real stories of real people (and businesses) that will fascinate you and further impress upon you the elements that work best to get the most for your business from your own Twitter presence.

■ ■ WHAT'S NOT IN THIS BOOK

Since this is a business- and communication-themed book, don't expect to find the sort of high-tech details that would promise to transform you into a full-blown Twitter technician. The focus here is how to angle a Twitter presence to benefit your business. As you'll soon read, Twitter success is firmly based on substance—concise though it may be—and not on style, so this book focuses squarely upon the key element of the content of your messages. While you'll learn how to use the Twitter toolset and do some fun customizing of your Twitter account and settings, that's as deep as we'll go, as this is about improving your business results, not your technical acumen.

■ ■ ■ Fly Me a Message—My Tweet

Naturally, the Internet, what with its various portals and places, remains a continually evolving entity. That said, expect that Twitter's main site might undergo some cosmetic or functional changes, new tools will certainly emerge, and even some new usage rules and guidelines might be passed down from Twitter HQ. Despite the many Twitter updates and upgrades that are sure to come, including those that occur once this book is published, this book is written to be as change-proof as possible and focuses on good business approaches *that will remain relevant in the face of any technical modifications*. Of course, technical changes to Twitter's platform *could* affect how you apply some of the techniques discussed herein, so if ever you find yourself with additional questions, please don't hesitate to drop me a line and inquire (if I haven't already answered your question with a tweet). This book will continue to serve you well, and you should be able to weather most site modifications, but if ever you find you've reached a slowing point and want to chat directly about applying the principles presented in this book, please contact me at dlprince@ bigfoot.com.

But now, turn the page and begin to understand how Twitter can be the freshest and most effective tool that will help you reach more customers (and new friends) in a way that is just as satisfying and meaningful for you as it will be for your audience. Let's get started.

PART 1

Understanding Twitter

1

Welcome to the World of Microblogging

THROUGHOUT HISTORY, PEOPLE HAVE felt compelled to speak out about whatever it is that launches them out of bed each morning, be it a product they are selling, a service they are offering, or a personal passion they would like to share with others. In days past, people would distribute their self-promotional messages via corner "barkers," leaflets shoved into any open hand that happened by, garish sandwich boards emblazoned with a pitch, and so forth. This sort of carnival appeal gave way to sophisticated messaging via the radio and television, on which those pitching had more time to craft an informative appeal and could reach thousands and millions of listeners or viewers in a vacuum-tube instant. When the computer age arrived, the message was mere keystrokes away, easy to construct, perfect, and transmit with a click of a "send" button.

Today, the battle for an audience's attention is being fought via *microblogging*, an electronically enabled communication method that allows a host, or microblogger, to broadcast quick but compelling bursts of data to subscribers of the microblog. *Microposts*, messages written to a microblog, can be made public on a website or distributed to a private group of subscribers. Subscribers can read microposts online or request that updates be delivered in real time to their computer desktop as an instant message or sent to a mobile device as an SMS (short message service) text message. In the world of microblogging, messages—the aforementioned microposts—generally range in length from 100 to 200 characters. Unlike the current outbreak of bombast and blather that comes as a din of information overload, be it via television, radio, or an electronic e-mail in-box flooded with unwanted appeals, microposts can provide a solution that serves the recipient as well as the sender in a way that brings even more efficiency and effectiveness to the message.

The standout name in microblogging by far is Twitter. The site has cut a new path right through the overgrowth of information excess, showing all a new way to speak and be heard. Because microposts are limited to lengths of just 140 characters or less, Twitter messages must be trim, concise, and easy to digest. Whether you want to tell others where you are, what you're doing, or what might await them if they simply follow your posts, Twitter makes it possible to get to the point and get down to the real business of communicating in a real and meaningful way. To the businessperson, Twitter enables a message that values the customer's time, offers immediacy of product or service availability, and helps establish a brand identity via brief but easy to remember messaging. And if you doubt that such a brief sort of communication can have any sort of lasting power within a customer's mind, consider the Nike Corporation's ubiquitous slogan, which consists of only three simple words: Just do it.

Microblogging works, and it can work for you and for your endeavors—as soon as today.

■ ■ ■ The Good Sense in Social Media

Before proceeding with the Twitter story, you might be wondering why Twitter matters. Isn't it just another of those social media time-wasters? And what's so great about "social media," anyway? Many consider it all a fad, blithely dismissing social media as just another lonely hearts club in a new digital domain. Honestly, what real value can come from all of this online interaction—writing on walls, "friending" others, sharing pictures and passions—that engages 110 million U.S. users daily? (That's an estimated 36 percent of the total population.) The fact is, social media has grown at an exponential rate, in a way that other traditional communication methods never achieved. Consider these statistics of communication-tool precursors in regard to the amount of time each required to reach 50 million users:

- Radio: 38 years
- Television: 13 years
- Internet: 4 years
- iPod: 3 years

Now consider that Facebook engaged 100 million users in less than nine months. Applications for the iPhone were accessed by one billion users in a same nine-month period. Twitter is on a similar growth path, as you'll read a bit later in this chapter. Clearly, social media is far more than just "social."

When it comes to the positive—some say explosive—impact of social media upon business and branding, consider these facts, sourced from Nielsen:

- 14 percent of consumers say they trust company-produced advertisements
- 18 percent of traditional TV ad campaigns generate positive returns on investment
- 25 percent of search results online for the world's top-twenty largest brands are links to user-generated (socially accessible) content
- 34 percent of bloggers post opinions about products and brands
- 78 percent of consumers trust peer recommendations

With that final bullet, it's clear that many turn to social networking sites and tools for more than mere social interaction. In fact, it has been determined that social networks and blogs now serve as the fourth most popular online activity, exceeding individuals' use of their own personal e-mail accounts. That said, it's clear that social media has been transformed in remarkably short order, proving the naysayers wrong when they asserted it was nothing more than a frivolous distraction with no resultant value. On the contrary, since social networking has become the communication method of choice for an emerging (and financially empowered) generation, it has become more than clear to astute businesses and brands that now is the time to migrate to this new arena where people are talking. Therefore, Nielsen's published studies have concluded:

- 88 percent of businesses have now indicated they are employing social media for marketing purposes
- 72 percent of businesses, however, have only been using social media marketing for less than six months (embracing the shift to where the audience is congregating)
- 81 percent of businesses say the number one benefit of social media sites and tools is generating company and brand exposure, followed by increasing traffic and building new relationships with peers and customers
- Over half of businesses that employed use of social media saw a rise in their search-engine rankings (recall the third bullet in the previous list)
- Of social-media tools marketers most wanted to learn about, Twitter ranked second-highest, following social bookmarking sites (such as Digg, reddit, and Delicious).

So if you thought social media amounts to simply another dalliance into developing personal popularity and nursing a low measure of self-esteem, think again. Truly, people are gathering and chatting, but they're chatting about much more than last night's date, last week's fashion faux pas, or last month's run-in with Mom and Dad. They're talking, all right, but they might be talking about you and your business—if you're there to be talked about.

■ ■ ■ Who Is Jack Dorsey, and Why Do You Care?

The notion of the messaging of one's "status" from one person to others—that being, what's the current situation, where are you, and what are you doing—came from the finger-drumming of programmer Jack Dorsey (see Figure 1-1). The Missouri-born Dorsey took interest in taxi-dispatch routing by the age of fourteen and went on to develop open-source software that is still in use at East Coast taxi-cab companies. Dorsey relocated to Oakland, California, in 2000 with aspirations of starting a company that would dispatch taxis, package couriers, and even emergency services from a Web-based hub. This concept attracted him to the LiveJournal.com site, where he further toyed with a concept of providing Web-based access to "status information" (no, not personal assets but rather information such as "where are you," "what are you doing," and "what's happening?").

Determining his vision could only be achieved if he blended traditional Web presence with the immediacy of instant messaging (such as was made rampantly popular through AOL's Instant Messenger tool),

Figure 1-1. Are you curious to know what a millennial billionaire is doing? If so, follow Twitter creator, cofounder, and chairman Jack Dorsey at http://twitter.com/jack.

he began conceiving a simple interface design through which, by his own definition, he could enable a truly "live" LiveJournal—real-time journal entries from wherever and whenever. Having joined Odeo, a Web 2.0 company whose site provides users with RSS-syndicated audio and video, he continued to work on his idea, slipping small bits of the potential solution into his projects there. Over the course of several years, he came to believe the idea was finally ready for prime time, and he pitched it to the receptive ears of then-creative director Isaac "Biz" Stone and investor Evan Williams. In March 2006, Dorsey sketched out the interface (see Figure 1-2), and within two short weeks, he had developed the initial functional design of Twitter, then named stat.us.

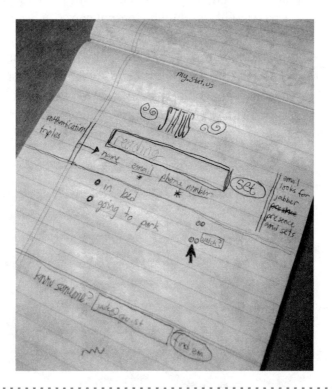

Figure 1-2. The doodles of a winning design: Jack Dorsey's original concept sketch. (Source: Jack Dorsey's Flickr photostream, open permission granted.)

■■■ A Session in Name-Storming

Since naming and branding are paramount when carving out and retaining public mindshare, Dorsey, Stone, and Williams knew their breakthrough status-messaging tool needed to have a high level of mental stickiness. Technical jargon sometimes fits the bill but typically only attracts an audience of like-minded tech junkies—especially if there's some technical in-joke embedded somewhere in the name. Wisely, these three entrepreneurs knew their target audience was much larger—all-encompassing, really—and the name had to have appeal, meaning, and retention for practically everyone in every field of interest. In a February 2009 *Los Angeles Times* interview, Jack Dorsey described it this way:

> So we did a bunch of name-storming, and we came up with the word "twitch," . . . but [it wasn't] a good product name because it doesn't bring up the right imagery. So we looked in the dictionary for words around it, and we came across the word "twitter," and it was just perfect. The definition was "a short burst of inconsequential information," and "chirps from birds." And that's exactly what the product was.

Of course, the original name reveals the natural tech instincts of Dorsey, who initially noted it as "twttr"—the five-character name being aligned with the American SMS short code naming convention while also borrowing a bit of the contraction style found in the name of the popular photo-sharing site Flickr. Ultimately, however, the name was expanded to Twitter. The service launched publicly in July 2006, and Twitter became a full-fledged company by May 2007. Today, Twitter is headquartered in the business district of San Francisco, nestled amid a working population that darts about to achieve the day's to-do list while always finding time to briefly connect and chat along the way, very much in the spirit of (and perhaps as a perpetual inspiration to) the Twitter philosophy.

And, to the original question posed at the beginning of this discussion—who is Jack Dorsey, and why do you care? Well, here's your answer: Jack Dorsey is important to you not because he created Twitter for your use. Rather, he is important to you because he created Twitter to fill a bona fide business need, via immediate and intelligent communication, to solve a problem and enhance a customer experience (that is, for those who are awaiting a taxicab, package delivery, or in need of emergency services). The importance of his motivation to create Twitter, real-time yet simple, is the same approach you should adopt to make the most of your business growth and customer experience through the tool's use.

Your task, going forward, is to apply the Jack Dorsey model of sensibility to your revised and improved outreach efforts today. As Jack did, identify any communication barriers that are hampering an aspect of your business or one of your personal goals and determine how the use of immediate, concise, and focused messaging might smooth the interaction you have with your customers, providing them useful—and possibly entertaining—information at up-to-the-minute availability. So, the new question is, When you begin to incorporate Twitter into your business strategy, will you have any Jack in you?

■■■ The Growth and Maturation of the Twitter Community

Now that you know more about Twitter, the company and its founders, it's time to understand the evolution of the service with regard to the folks who use it, many of whom now claim they can't live without it. Since its inception, the site has attracted users from all backgrounds and with varying needs and intents, which sounds like the recipe for widespread adoption, businesswise. For some early users, Twitter emerged as that aforementioned relief from the e-mail onslaught and as a way to reach many recipients ("followers") more quickly than is possible with traditional e-mail transmissions. Others were less than impressed, countering that it would prove itself to be just another handheld cultural distraction that would only attract the mindless and meandering youth of this inconsequential information-indulgent age, eager to click and cluck their time away. It didn't take long, however, for the Twitter team to silence those who fell into the latter camp.

Indeed, during the 2007 South by Southwest (SXSW) festival, a series of interactive and media conferences held annually in Austin, Texas, the Twitter team in attendance powered up large, 60-inch plasma-screen monitors and used them to display the stream of messages authored by attendees, who used the service to actively keep in touch with one another's activities and whereabouts as the festival ran. The immediacy of the information coupled with the novel method of delivery made Twitter the surprise hit of the festival, and tweet traffic jumped from twenty thousand messages per day to sixty thousand, solidifying the foundation upon which the service was being built and would continue to grow. The results of this South by Southwest festival were telling in that they demonstrated the true audience for the Twitter methodology, and young and old, those most receptive to its value have continued to make good use of its benefits, both sending and receiving.

Since that South by Southwest festival, Twitter's user base has grown exponentially. According to Nielsen Online, people around the globe have been spending more and more time in "social networking" endeavors, be that on traditional blogs and networking sites or within the emerging microblogging realm. In the first half of 2009, Nielsen charted that total minutes spent in social networking had increased 82 percent year over year for all users surveyed with the average time each person spends networking having increased 67 percent year over year. As for Twitter, it was recognized as the fastest growing Web brand as of May 2009, realizing a staggering 1,448 percent increase year over year, with its user base growing from 1.2 million unique visitors in May 2008 to 18.2 million in May 2009. Moreover, average time spent at Twitter per person had increased 175 percent, from 6 minutes 19 seconds in May 2008 to 17 minutes 21 seconds in May 2009. Within those growing statistics are millions of ears and eyes searching for relevant and rewarding experiences, the sort of folks you might want to connect with if you have the product, service, or experience these people are actively seeking.

Now for an even more interesting statistic: although Twitter was charted as the fastest growing brand during the first half of 2009, its monthly growth showed a bit of tapering off within that same period, leveling a bit as some of its faddish newness had begun to wane a bit. Sure, it became the hit with celebrities, newscasters, and even presidential candidates, enticing millions of citizens to flock to it to rub virtual elbows with the red carpet crowd, but when the fanfare passes, so too do some of the fair-weather followers.

Is this bad news a negative trend for Twitter? Arguably, no. The trends show that just as other successful and sustaining social network hubs, such as Facebook, are working to retain (and attract) a committed audience, so too is Twitter. After the fan-boys and girls have scampered to the next "cool place to be," the wise among the users will have learned that developing a lasting relationship with a committed audience is more beneficial than fruitlessly striving to maintain the attention of the bubblegum crowd. Businesspeople have learned to engage in these sorts of technologies early and then to stick around to reap the benefits of the toolset long after the Hello Kitty kids have gone. This isn't to disparage the youth—they're a viable and important segment to understand and entertain—but a lasting endeavor builds upon a loyal audience. To continually chase the flashbulb-popping contingent is to waste time and money continually reinventing to the new flavor of the month. Make sense?

■ ■ ■ The Real Value of the Tweet: It's Not Just About "What's Happening?"

Having read this far, you could be wondering to yourself, "Why do I care what someone else is doing right now, who they're standing next to, and what brand of granola they've just eaten for breakfast?" Excellent question—this is where the opportunity of Twitter begins to emerge for each person that begins to give it serious consideration, especially within the realm of business or personal benefit. The truth is, the value of Twitter isn't expressed by the concept of "What are you doing?" and "What's happening?"—not literally, anyway.

If you wonder whether any 140-character blurb can be of much impact or lasting value, you could have a valid argument. In fact, that imposed constraint does seem as if it would cut short any enticing message just as it was getting started. Actually, no—the audience has grown weary of long-winded harangues and wants to know, within seconds, if what you have to say is worth hearing (or reading). This puts the onus back on the messenger, forcing a meaningful approach with a sentence or two—and this is good. Why? Simply enough, the messenger must become both text- and time-efficient, saying more in less space. Imagine if you could cut your business's marketing budget in half or by three-fourths simply by focusing your message and establishing the same impact in less space utilized. That would be the sort of cost savings that would likely gain you accolades around the office, right? Twitter *forces* that efficiency, and, whether you're initially amenable to it or not, you *will* need to comply to the constraint. After a short while, you will have retrained yourself to think more concisely and message more precisely; it's unavoidable.

If you still argue that it is impossible to craft a persuasive message using only 140 characters, that's fine, because in actuality, you're not constrained at all. Picture traveling down a road where, a short way ahead, is the most remarkable fruit stand in this part of the county. About a mile before the turnoff, you see a sign: "Looking for something really fresh?" Maybe you are, maybe you aren't, but either way you're curious what this is about. About fifty yards farther, you see a second sign: "It should be illegal, it's so good." Now you're intrigued. Further on you read: "We invite you to pinch, poke, and thump." And so you get the idea that this leads to a hidden oasis of fruits and vegetables that are simply to die for. You've probably already figured out that careful stringing of Twitter messages, or tweets, can achieve the same result if it's carefully conceived and doesn't prolong the final payoff. If you're particularly talented at this sort of "leading," you could develop an audience of followers who love your message as much as what it is you offer. (Ever watch the Super Bowl just for the sake of enjoying the inventive advertisements?)

But getting back to the assertion that Twitter isn't just about "what are you doing" and "what's happening," consider these examples of how tweets were adapted to tell about more than the whipped cream and mocha dust on this morning's latte:

- As a talent recruitment tool, some companies post job openings on Twitter, especially those in need of specialized talent. Equally, companies monitor tweets from the Twitter community to locate those who have key talents to offer and are actively seeking employment.
- As a customer survey tool, some businesses ask the Twitterverse for opinions about a recently released product or service (or ask about the lasting value of an existing offering). Similarly, savvy businesses are scanning posted tweets for chatter—good or bad—about their products or services and then are responding in kind.
- As a real-time coordination tool, many folks use Twitter to organize spontaneous business gatherings—also known as *tweetups*—perhaps to address a troublesome business problem, to brainstorm a fast plan for a new opportunity, or just to gather a business team for some well-deserved downtime.
- And, as a "capacity maximization" tool, a San Francisco health spa utilized Twitter to tweet about same-day appointment opportunities and discounts to folks, who took up the open appointment windows; it was better than having no clients (or revenue) for those otherwise unused time slots.

This is just the start of the story—the leading tweet, if you will. As you read along in this book, you'll discover how to look at Twitter in a refreshing new way, not for pure exploitation but rather for effective engagement of the Twitterverse. As you'll learn, the key to tweeting is to first understand and respect the using community. Yes, you'll be using the tool for a business-relevant purpose (by the nature of this book), but that doesn't mean you'll strive to drown out the rest of the tweets with harsh sales pitches; quite the opposite, really. The potential of Twitter is that it enables you to become truly personable in your engagement of associates and customers, which in turn affords you a more concise view of what you offer, how you offer it, and how you listen to those who like or dislike it. In the next chapter, you'll read about the keys to a useful and beneficial Twitter approach, and you'll be prompted to begin thinking—or rethinking—how you'll engage your target audience. You may even discover there's an audience out there that you never considered before.

2

Planning for Twitter in Your Business

NOW THAT YOU HAVE an understanding of the Twitter platform—where it came from and, more important, *why* it was created, it's time to take a look at your aspirations, business or personal, to determine how you'll put Twitter to work for you. That's right—in order to break the oft-bemoaned stigma that these social networking tools are just a personal time drain, you'll need to commit now to the idea that Twitter will be a tool that will offer benefits to you, rather than wind up as a distraction that keeps you from running your business. In this chapter, you'll jump into the important task of *defining* Twitter for your needs: what it will do, what it won't do, and how you can make the most out of your time investment in it. Since time is one of the greatest investments each of us has to offer a business or other such pursuit, the time you devote to harnessing, evolving, and maintaining a Twitter presence needs to be thought out far in advance. So, before getting into the details of how to create a Twitter account and how to begin tweeting, this chapter will help you consider—as did Jack Dorsey—*why* you'd use Twitter in your business and how that use would help you realize your goals.

■ ■ ■ What Will Twitter Do for You?

As you read in Chapter 1, Twitter offers easy, real-time communication between people. It allows an immediacy that keeps people in touch as they experience the day, discussing their likes, dislikes, wants, and needs. On the personal level, tweets are tantamount to the sort of chitchat that happens over a cup of coffee—friends and associates sharing their thoughts and ideas as they occur. To the business mind, this is the sort of treasured interaction and unbridled feedback that are highly valued and deeply regarded (by those who know how to listen to the voice of the customer, anyway). If you had direct and immediate access to your customers' thoughts and attitudes, you'd be in the best position to monitor

- who your customers are.
- why these customers have decided to use/consume your product or service.
- what your customers like—and don't like—about your product or service.
- how your customers respond to adjustments in your offerings (or those of your competitors).
- how influential your customers might be in convincing—or dissuading—others regarding your offerings.

This is just the beginning, of course, but through the use of Twitter, you tend to gain that coveted "fly on the wall" proximity to see and hear what others are saying about you, your business, and your products. With this information, you can establish and adjust your business approach at the "speed of business" to align with the more-rapid-than-ever changing consumer sentiments. Twitter in your business, then, gives you access to this valuable feedback—via direct communication or through cross-chatter among users who are actively tweeting back and forth on your Twitter page. Take a look at the Starbucks Coffee tweet stream in Figure 2-1 and see how they're tweeting about "free pastry day" while also getting immediate information about a

Figure 2-1. How's the coffee? Did you get today's coupon? Did you know today is "free pastry day"? These are just a few of the tantalizing tweets from Starbucks Coffee.

less-than-stellar customer service situation (one that can be corrected immediately, thanks to the tweets).

The Starbucks Coffee example demonstrates how Twitter enables a *high-touch* interaction between the business and its customers, allowing a more focused relationship to develop than might otherwise emerge in a usual over-the-counter interaction. In fact, if a customer had been left dissatisfied in a traditional store setting, it's possible that individual could have caused a commotion at the counter that surely would have been seen and heard by those waiting in line to place their orders as well as by those in the nearby seating area. This is the sort of situation a business owner or operator wants to address quickly, but he or she will also need to work quickly to soothe the environment for the other patrons (after all, a place like Starbucks is built upon its casual and comfortable setting).

Worse still, had that dissatisfied customer been unable or unwilling to call direct attention to the problem, it's just as likely that individual would have left the store without indicating the matter to anyone, possibly never to return again—which would result in lost business. Either way, the high-tech yet high-touch connection that Twitter offers can sometimes mend ways between customers and business owners. This isn't to suggest that a business should post notice to the effect of "all complaints should be tweeted to http://twitter.com/wewillget backtoyou," but Twitter does offer a viable alternative for customers to share their experiences, good and bad, directly with the business. For you and your business, this is one method of open communication to consider, and if you implement it, it's one you'll want to monitor closely and respond to at regular and reliable intervals.

■ ■ ■ Using Twitter for Tracking and Redirecting

As was previously mentioned, tracking your customers' thoughts and ideas via interactive tweeting is of the utmost importance. Indeed, you can achieve incredible gains and solid credibility with your customers if you're able to understand and respond to their needs in a real-time manner. This element of tracking allows you to keep a pulse on your customers' activity and gives you the opportunity to adjust and adapt—or just keep doing all of the good things you're currently doing—based upon the tweets you receive. If you operate a business that has multiple brick-and-mortar locations, you might track why one store seems to be busier than another—in the Starbucks example, maybe the music is better, there are more copies of the morning paper to read, or perhaps there's proper screening of an otherwise blinding morning sun. By tracking, you can see where your business is flourishing and where it isn't, and then determine what improvements need to be implemented at the less-traveled location.

Through tracking, you can also keep a pulse on your customers' experience during their visit and add a bit of additional entertainment during their stay. In Figure 2-2, Popeye's Chicken is having some good fun with their Twitter followers by offering a virtual "hug of thanks and appreciation" to those who are enjoying their meals and then asking them the proverbial riddle, "Why did the chicken cross the road?" Followers are asked to post their best explanations to the question by "FRYday" of the week, adding an element of interactivity to Popeye's tweets. It's simple, it's fun, and it shows the customers and follow-

Figure 2-2. Why did the chicken cross the road? That's what Popeye's Chicken is asking you in their fun and engaging Twitter feed.

ers that Popeye's Chicken is all about having a good time over a tasty meal.

When you track customers via Twitter, you can learn what's working for them and what isn't, which will help you modify your approach on the fly, so to speak. And while you wouldn't want to be in perpetual reaction mode, jerking to and fro to any customer's whim, you can address the immediate issues (customer service and such) while collecting the rest of the input to check for trends or shifts in attitude—and this begs exploration of the method of *directing* your customers.

It has been a longtime business tenet that good marketing involves developing a product or message, establishing a need within the recipient's mind, and then directing a response by motivating the recipient to act, whether by visiting an establishment, purchasing a product, or praising a company to a friend. For an established Twittering business, Twitter contributes to that approach as follows:

- It affords the business the opportunity to get to know its customers through tracking, as previously noted.
- Through its tracking efforts, the business can identify the trends that have captured the attention of its customer base. It can then adjust its sales strategy accordingly and offer its customers more of what they like, correct those aspects of its products that they dislike, and pinpoint which of their needs have not yet been fulfilled.
- After analyzing the feedback of its customers and factoring in their likes and dislikes, the business can determine the best product or service it can offer that will uphold the spirit of "we listen to you."
- After releasing its new offering, the business should resume tracking to determine if the new offering has hit the mark and is successful.

Beyond this, the already-Twittering business can utilize the feedback and strong customer ties to suggest new products or services not yet asked for but which seem suited to the base. For example, if you operate a restaurant or other such gathering place and always notice folks tweeting across your page about the big game that's coming up (and they're planning to depart in time to watch it), this is an easy cue to install monitors so they can watch from your establishment. You also can offer game-time specials and other such promotions to draw them in and cause them to make plans to return to your establishment when the next game airs. Conversely, if you've satisfied this opportunity but read tweets that indicate it's too noisy for folks to have a conversation, maybe it's time to adjust the volume some or establish a somewhat segregated and slightly quieter area for those not interested in the play-by-play events.

Within the realm of consumer goods—computer equipment, to be precise—consider how Dell Inc., formerly Dell Computer, has utilized Twitter to straddle both the tracking and directing sides of the customer engagement approach. Their Twitter page is designed as a hub of information and access for customers, offering technical updates, customer service access, and social networking avenues that allow Dell customers (and perhaps soon-to-be customers) to interact with one another as well as Dell representatives with regard to computers and technology.

If you study the Dell page of Twitter links in Figure 2-3, you might conclude it's not very Twitter-like—and you'd be right. It does take an extreme approach to Twitter-for-business, but it's useful in demonstrating the high-side potential that Twitter offers, allowing a business to establish multiple Twitter accounts to more closely address specific customer wants and needs. While this approach might seem to lack that social feel of connectedness (that is, it's a significant collection of specialized links that doesn't quite embody the casual mood of a Twitter interaction), it nevertheless offers a multitude of access points to information, shopping, and service from a consolidated hub. Your task, as you establish your Twitter approach for your business, will be to find a happy medium between the too casual social-for-social's-sake approach and the potentially overdone business-for-business's-sake alternative, developing a Twitter presence that allows you to interact with your customers in a friendly manner while sensibly serving your targeted customers' needs along the way.

Figure 2-3. Do you have a question or some feedback? Or perhaps you want to shop for the latest computer deals? You can do it all from the various Dell pages at Twitter. From this page on the Dell.com site, you'll find numerous links to Twitter accounts to guide you in buying closeout goods, getting technical assistance, and gaining interaction in region-specific matters.

■■■Are You Convinced Yet?

By now you should begin pondering the previous examples of how various businesses use Twitter, as well as how you'll develop your own approach for your business or endeavor. As you can see, you're only limited by your creativity, imagination, and willingness to establish your own identity (or that of your business) within the Twitter-verse. What if you're still not convinced? Sure, it's conceivable that the questions just answered have conjured up additional misgivings or moments for pause and even hesitations about whether or not Twitter is truly a useful tool for business. Even if you haven't conceived your own list of potential drawbacks or reservations about the tool, others have.

Here are some of the most common arguments given against use of Twitter in business:

- **It requires a strategy, a purpose, staffing, and time.** Of course it does; so does any other worthwhile business strategy. The good news is that it's easy to create an account and to begin tweeting within minutes. The time and effort invested could pay handsome dividends and would tally only a fraction of the cost of "traditional" market research and customer-survey methods (especially those managed by third-party firms).

- **It's another investment into customer service; it's redundant.** Well, if you ask your customers, they'll likely tell you there aren't enough ways to express their feelings about your products or services, good or bad. While it's true that a well-staffed customer service team cannot be fully replaced (and if you think so, just watch your customers' exodus to a competitor), Twitter offers what the now-tired FAQ approach doesn't—interaction. The FAQ still serves a purpose, but it limits customers to only the information provided, and as we all know, one answer does not fit all variations of a question. Twitter allows a new method to respond to customer inquiries without the need for a costly phone bank. And, often several customers can chime in to a tweeted question, allowing the business to respond to multiple customers in one reply (or quickly redirect them to the best information for their needs).

- **Twitter is still growing and hasn't fully stabilized yet.** As of this writing, that's partly true, yet how reliable are the old-fashioned "suggestion boxes" that many businesses still insist will be suitable for collecting customer feedback? The fact is, it's important to make the most of these sorts of social tools early to establish a following and identity as the service itself grows and matures. Surely Twitter wouldn't be your only method of customer outreach and interaction, but by the same token, why would you ignore it on merit of its newness?

- **Twitter is just for those tech geeks.** Actually, tech is every-where, and folks from hardened nerds to soccer moms are using it for their own needs. Information and interaction are always top-ranking attractions for customers; a new tool simply keeps up with progress.

- **Twitter is just another social fad.** If you believe this argu-ment, then you're bound to struggle in reaping the most for your business. Employed effectively, as you'll find described in this book, Twitter used for business purposes dispenses with the cyber-babble yammering from many and helps target folks truly serious about you, your business, and your offerings. If targeted marketing, customer interaction, and informed product and service develop-ment are fads, then long live the fad!

You've probably heard several variations on these "problems" with using Twitter for your business, but as you can see, they fall some-what flat in their assertions. The greatest buoy for arguing in Twitter's favor is that it was built upon the solid need for fast and frequent interaction (again, recalling Jack Dorsey's taxi dispatch solution). Communication, fast and fluid, is what helps some businesses excel past their competitors. Provided the business is truly interested in hearing what customers have to say and is committed to responding to their questions and concerns in a thoughtful and sensible manner, then Twitter is merely another way to reach customers. All customers wish they could be treated as if they're the only one who matters; with Twitter, we're closer than ever to that possibility.

■■■ Playing the Name Game—Carefully

As you're evolving your vision of how you'll use Twitter in your busi-ness and what it is you'll tweet, it's time to pause and consider *who* you'll be at Twitter. While the discussion of your Twitter "personality" will come a bit later in this book, this is the time to carefully consider your chosen name on Twitter. Will yours be representative of your business, engaging to your followers, and memorable to all who will eagerly—and hopefully *easily*—remember you by your Twitter name? Selecting your Twitter user name is a very important step, but it's fun, too.

You'll probably hear your Twitter name referred to as a "handle"—just like the high-riding, horn-blowing truckers who have chatted back and forth over their CB radios using handles like Rubberduck and Pig Pen. Your Twitter handle becomes the way your followers can get in touch with you, track your tweets, and interact with you (or your business). For that reason, you will want a handle or name that is easy to remember and reflects who you are and what it is that you do. If you're in the business of selling rubber ducks, for example, then Rubberduck is a preferred name. If someone else has already taken the name you want (and, by this point in Twitter's existence, it is largely possible you won't get your first choice of names), consider an alternate name that conveys the same idea but also differentiates you from others, such as Retrorubberduck or Weboduckies. You'll likely need to brainstorm numerous names, determining which on your list of good names would best represent what it is you hope to achieve on Twitter. Think about each name for a day or two and see which ones seem to stick in your mind the best.

Choosing a name can be agonizing to some folks, fearful of the fallout should they choose a "bad" one. Here's a list of considerations while you work to select a perfect Twitter handle:

- Try to select a short Twitter name (shorter than the 15-character Twitter-imposed limit if possible) for ease in typing, recall, and including within already-trim 140-character tweets.
- Select a name that's appropriate in an open forum. Avoid uncomfortable innuendo. Keep it appropriate for all ages in all settings.
- If you already have a business name or website, try to select a name that's similar or at least complementary to what you've already established.

- Avoid words that could easily be misspelled by your followers.
- Avoid adding numerals to your Twitter name since these can often be forgotten or mistyped by followers.
- Avoid dashes, underscores, and other special punctuation, since these characters are almost always mishandled by others online.

Remember, your Twitter name is your microblogging calling card, so devise and decide upon a name that's as functional to your purpose as it is fun for you and your followers. If it makes sense, is easy to remember and type, and is relevant to your intentions at Twitter, yours will be a handle that helps bolster your business.

▪▪▪ Legal Implications in Tweeting

Now, if you're one who fears that a lawyer is lurking just around the corner, ready to dredge up a "victim" and lay a profit-evaporating allegation against your brand or business, then perhaps the increased exposure you would otherwise enjoy from tweeting might be just the sort of thing to cause you restless nights. All facetiousness aside, every business and brand needs to have an awareness of some of the legal ramifications of marketing a product or service and the potential liabilities that come with the endeavor. Even with the freedom of access and interaction that Twitter provides, there's always a need to understand how "what you say might be used against you in a court of law." No, this isn't intended to be a Miranda-laden buzzkill to your creative momentum but rather just a friendly reminder that whatever you say on Twitter might not necessarily *stay* on Twitter. Naturally, you'd want to seek professional legal advice and representation for your business's protection, but in the meantime, here are some aspects of Twitter, from a legal perspective, that you should ponder:

- **Libel.** If you say something disparaging in a public forum about another individual or company, you could be held accountable. Since your tweets have the potential to reach millions of individuals, an aggressive claim for damages could be extensive. Of course even the most eager plaintiff would need to bear a substantial burden of proof, but even if such an allegation proved unsubstantiated, the legal costs, not to mention cost to your reputation, could be sizable. For this reason, take care in what you tweet about and how you tweet so your intent cannot ever be misconstrued as libelous against another person or entity (and that goes for any employees you might have who would tweet on your company's behalf).

- **Sharing privileged or confidential information.** This is typically a situation in which a company employee or representative might tweet about sensitive or legally protected information. Confidential information about a company or its partnerships that is leaked by a tweet could have severe ramifications, especially if a breach of contract or agreement occurs. Again, because each tweet has the potential to be seen by millions of users, the fallout could be significant. Ensure you understand the sensitivity of what you tweet about *before* you post your message.

- **Record-keeping requirements.** In many business settings, "record retention" requirements mandate that certain information be archived and kept available for inspection for a specified period of years. When it comes to promoting and selling products and services, it's important to understand (through legal counsel as well as local and federal business-operation regulations) what information is to be maintained. Because Twitter and social-media messaging is relatively new, the parameters here are evolving. Even so, it's in your best interest to maintain reliable records of your business-based tweeting. You might be called upon to provide the records of your messaging, and it's in your best interest if *you* can provide the details rather than be at the mercy of others who might present the information *as they see it*.

- **Use in litigation.** The statutes surrounding social media and the messaging therein are still applicable, and in some cases, this new form of online communication could be deemed inadmissible in a litigation setting. Even so, as noted in the previous point, consider a reliable record-keeping method for your business-centric tweeting just in case it could serve as the "star witness" to save the day.

With all that has been suggested, make sure you understand your responsibilities as a business owner, locally and at the federal level, as you go about doing business—even on Twitter. Seek out reliable legal advice on how you can make the most of your tweeting without straying into the fringe areas of all that is legal and permissible. Again, don't let this discussion dissuade you, but rather use it to ensure you are legally covered with respect to your usage of Twitter.

■ ■ ■ Twitter Restrictions, Rules, and Policies

Last, as you further consider and formulate the adoption of Twitter to your business, be certain your approach works within the tool's published rules of use and user-agreement boundaries. Don't worry—the parameters aren't so restrictive that they'll prevent you from making the most of the tool to your business's benefit, but there are some key regulations to be certain you understand and incorporate into your approach.

While you can always visit the "help" site and review the rules and policies directly at http://help.twitter.com/home (see Figure 2-4), here are the key points to understand:

Content Boundaries
- **Impersonation.** It is against Twitter rules to create an account for the purposes of posing as (impersonating) another individual, whether a celebrity or private citizen.
- **Threats.** Naturally, using Twitter to broadcast threats or violent intent is not tolerated.
- **Copyrighted material.** As with any public forum, republication or repurposing of copyrighted material by

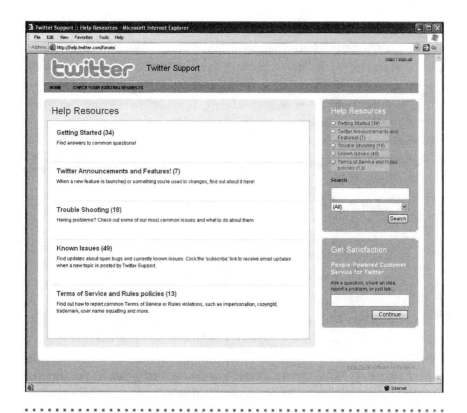

Figure 2-4. Visit the Twitter help portal for the latest updates to rules, regulations, and usage policies.

anyone other than the copyright owner is not allowed without express permission of the copyright holder.

- **User privacy.** It's against Twitter rules to broadcast private information about another individual (for example, private e-mail address, physical address, phone number).

Spam and Abuse

- **Serial accounts.** The practice of establishing multiple consecutive accounts for the sake of high-volume broadcasting is not allowed.

- **Name-squatting.** Securing user names without intent to actually use them, especially names that would be intended to sell to a more suitable user (for example, ParamountPictures) is not allowed.
- **Selling user names.** As indicated above, securing user account names for the purposes of selling them to a more suitable user is not allowed.
- **Phishing.** You may not publish links in your tweets that lead to spoof sites for the intention of illicitly gathering a person's information for unlawful or malicious use.
- **Spam.** Of course, the creation of accounts to be used for sending a barrage of unwanted messages to other users is not allowed (and the policies for identifying spamming within Twitter will continue to evolve as illicit users devise new methods of spamming).
- **Pornography.** No pornographic material may be transmitted or posted on a user's Twitter home page.

It's time for you to consider your business approach, your goals, and how using Twitter's real-time messaging can improve your results. Customer outreach and interaction has never been more important than now, and with Twitter, the gap that previously existed in this regard has become significantly smaller. Don't worry so much about giving the perception that your business is "hip" or "current" with the technology; that is faddism. Instead, use a solid business approach and consider Twitter as something as revolutionary as the telephone or the Internet. Adopt the tool, adapt it to your business (not the other way around), and get ready to engage your customers like never before.

PART 2

Establishing and Tweaking Your Twitter Presence

3

Joining Twitter and
Getting Started

WITH MUCH OF THE what-and-why discussion behind us, it's time to pick up some momentum and dive into the Twitter experience. If you've used online tools in the past to extend your brand (a website or Yahoo! Store, perhaps), alternate channels to help sell your products (maybe eBay or Amazon.com), or social networking sites to help spread the word (like MySpace), you'll be happy to know that setup at Twitter is remarkably fast and simple. As you read this and subsequent chapters, you will find brisk, guided discussions on account creation, sending of messages, as well as plenty of opportunities to pause a moment and consider your purpose at each step. So, without further ado, let's get you started.

Creating a Twitter Account

Open your favorite Web browser application and navigate to http://
twitter.com. When you arrive, you'll be greeted by the friendly and
simple home page (as shown in Figure 3-1). As simplicity is the theme
at Twitter, it's easy for newcomers to find the "Sign up now" button
at the right side of the home page screen. As an enticement as well
as convenience, you'll also see active links to the "popular topics by
the minute, day, and week." Thankfully, the site is free from cluttering
banners, ads, and other such mess that convolutes the message of
simplicity; hopefully Twitter can remain this way. With nothing much
more to see on Twitter's home page, feel free to click the Sign Up
Now button.

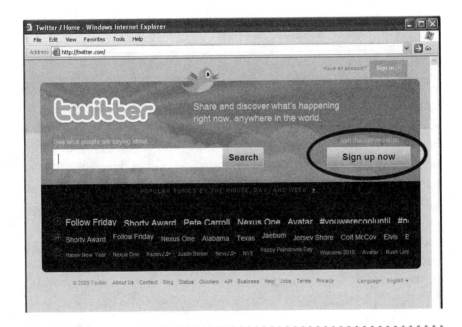

Figure 3-1. You'll discover that the Twitter home page is simple
and unassuming yet becomes a powerful portal to increasing
your outreach.

Upon clicking the Sign Up Now button from the Twitter home page, you'll navigate to one of the simplest sign-up screens in Internet history. All you need to provide, as highlighted in the numbered callouts in Figure 3-2, is the following:

1. **Your name.** No mystery here, it's just your name. Twitter will provide immediate feedback if your name is already in use in an existing active account (if so, it recognizes you've already created an account under your name, or—gulp—someone else has).

2. **Your desired user name.** Here's where you create the user name that folks within the Twitterverse will come to know you by. For the purposes of an example, I'm creating a new Twitter account, mywayback, which will result in a new Twitter URL of http://twitter. com/mywayback. Again, Twitter will check its database to determine if the user name you've specified is available or not. Oh, be advised that the site does not allow the use of "twitter" or "twttr" within user names.

3. **Your password.** To create a very strong password, ensure it's more than six characters long and includes a combination of letters, numbers, special characters, and capital and lowercase letters. If it's so cryptic that you earn the "very strong" indicator (as I have), write it down somewhere until you're certain you've committed it to memory.

4. **Your e-mail address.** A valid e-mail address is all you need. Twitter will check to see if an account already exists with the e-mail address you specify, though.

Upon entering that information, you'll need to type in the stylized characters you see in the "captcha" security string (see callout 5 in Figure 3-2); this prevents automated software applications from being able to create multiple accounts for spam or other illicit purposes. And before you click the Create My Account button, you can elect to review the terms of service details (these are the rules and regulations you'll be agreeing to when you use Twitter) by clicking the active text link (see callout 6 in Figure 3-2). So, click the button and create your account.

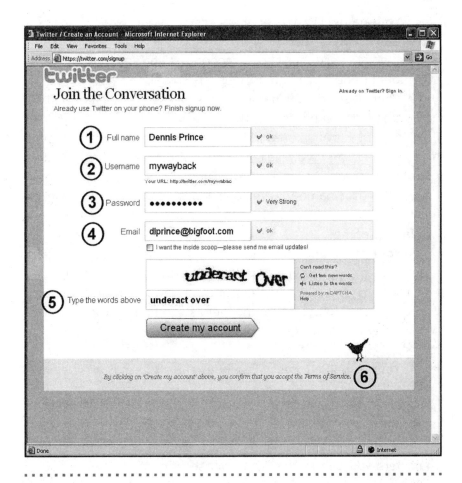

Figure 3-2. You are only required to enter a few fields of information to create your Twitter account.

Now, before you actually can complete your account activation, Twitter will take you on a bit of a detour. First you will be asked if you have any friends with e-mail accounts at Google (Gmail), Yahoo, or AOL (see Figure 3-3).

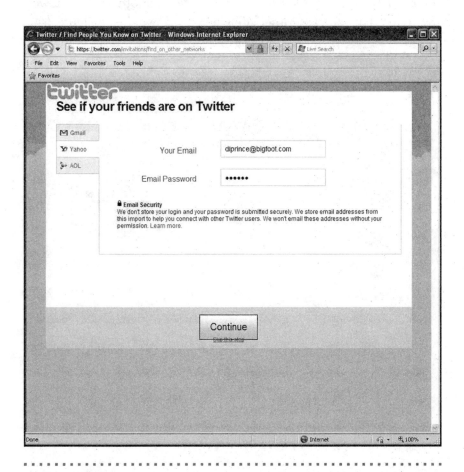

Figure 3-3. Use this screen to see if you have friends who might already be using Twitter.

If you do, you can click the appropriate icons to access those services and see if any of your friends already have their own Twitter accounts. If you wish, you can click the Skip This Step text link at the bottom of the screen. Next, you'll be directed to another screen that offers twenty preselected Twitter users of fame or otherwise noteworthy status that you can immediately begin following (see Figure 3-4).

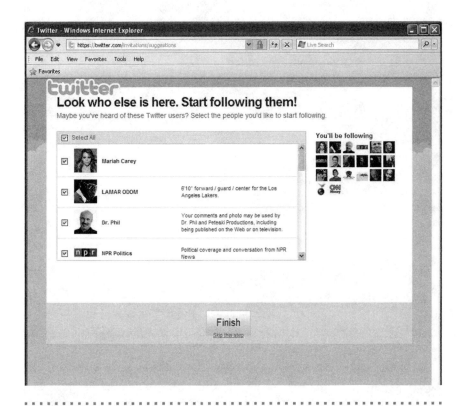

Figure 3-4. If you want to start following some of the more active or notable Twitter users, this screen suggests twenty of them for you.

You can deselect any or all of these suggested users that you don't wish to follow. If you click the Finish button, the users you have left as selected will be added to your list of users you're following. If you click the Skip This Step link at the bottom of the page, the twenty users will not be included as accounts you're following.

Finally, after navigating past the two detour screens, you will arrive at the account completion screen where you're already invited to launch your first tweet (see Figure 3-5).

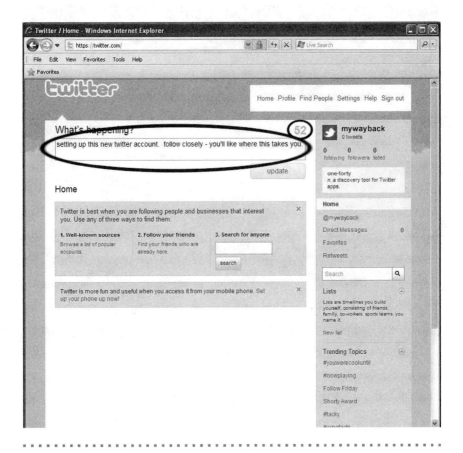

Figure 3-5. You've successfully set up your Twitter account; it's time to tweet.

Type in a tweet in the box labeled "What's happening?" (see Figure 3-6). To the right of that label, you'll see a counter that decreases as you type, letting you easily see how many characters you have left to use. When your message is complete, simply click the Update button (since you've now updated folks about what you're doing). After you have sent your first tweet, Twitter will refresh your home screen to show your first tweet; it's that easy.

Figure 3-6. Upon your first tweet, you'll see this refreshed home page that indicates your message.

You'll notice Twitter is also prompting you to do a couple more things from this screen. Item 2 in the on-screen list invites you to "follow your friends"; this is the same function that you saw previously when you were creating your account (refer to Figure 3-3). If you're not certain which of your friends might already be using Twitter, item 3 provides a search box where you can type in your friends' names and search to find them. Most notable, however, is the unnumbered item just below the numbered functions that encourages you to link your Twitter account to your mobile phone number, allowing you to send and receive tweets when you're away from your computer. Click on the text link "Set up your phone now!" and you'll navigate to the "Mobile" screen, which is actually an element of your overall site settings. Figure 3-7 shows how the process begins with sending a text message to Twitter from your mobile device. From there, the process will proceed as detailed in the next few paragraphs following Figure 3-7.

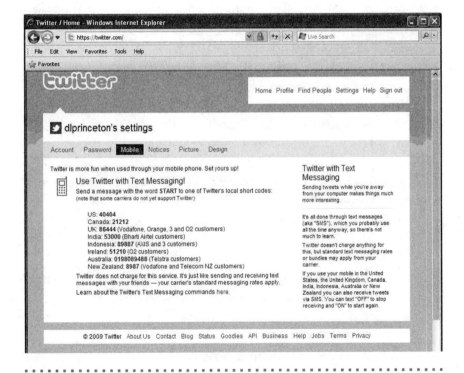

Figure 3-7. When you're ready to receive tweets on your mobile device, navigate to the "Mobile" screen from your account Settings to activate a link to your mobile phone number.

- **Send a text message to Twitter from your mobile device.** As you see in Figure 3-7, Twitter provides the text codes for you to send a text message with the word "START." Since I'm located in the United States, Twitter specifies I send my message to 40404. Short codes for other countries are listed as well.
- **Receive a response on your mobile device from Twitter.** The message Twitter sends to your device instructs you to reply with a message of "SIGNUP" to continue the process.
- **Receive another response on your mobile device from Twitter.** Now you're asked to respond with your Twitter user name. Here's where you actually link your mobile device to your account.
- **Receive yet another response on your mobile device from Twitter.** At this point, Twitter should recognize your account name (provided you entered it correctly in your previous text message response) indicating the account name already exists—this is good because you're establishing a linkage to your existing account. Twitter instructs you to respond with "ITS MINE" to verify the account is yours.
- **Receive a next response on your mobile device from Twitter.** This time, you're asked to respond with your Twitter account password. This is the verification step to assure you're the account owner.
- **Receive still another response on your mobile device from Twitter.** If Twitter recognizes your password from the previous step, this message requests that you respond with "OK" to complete the linkage of your mobile device to your Twitter account. You're nearly done with the process.
- **Receive a final response on your mobile device from Twitter.** Lastly, Twitter provides a confirmation message that your mobile device is linked to your account and ready to use. Good job.

With that, you're in. You're a registered Twitter user, you have access via a mobile device, and you're ready to begin tweeting. But wait, not so fast. There are still a few more things you can do to better communicate your Twitter persona to your followers. Read on now to see what else awaits you.

■ ■ ■ Navigating the Remaining Site Functions

Assuming you've since exited Twitter, returning to your account is easy. Simply go to twitter.com and log in to your active account in the area noted in Figure 3-8.

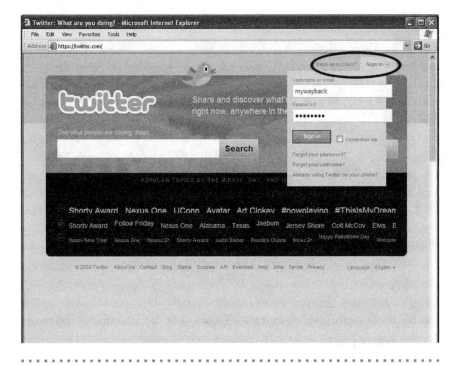

Figure 3-8. When you return to Twitter, log in to your account from this area on the site home page.

Upon logging in, your browser will navigate you to *your* home page at Twitter. As illustrated in Figure 3-9, your Twitter home page is your Web-based hub to launch tweets, monitor responses, and also modify your page settings and account information.

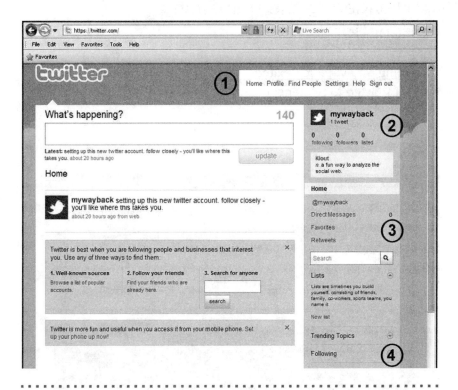

Figure 3-9. Your personal Twitter home page includes access to all areas needed to manage and maintain your account.

By the numbered callouts in Figure 3-9, here's what's on your Twitter home page:

1. The convenient site navigation menu ("navmenu" or "navbar") gives you easy access to the different areas where you can manage your account and page settings.

2. Your account statistics give you an easy view of how many other users you're following, how many are following you, and how many tweets ("updates") you've broadcast.
3. Your home statistics indicate how many replies have been sent to you via the "@mywayback" direct-messaging method (more about this in Chapter 5), the number of direct messages you've sent to other users, and any favorite messages and messengers you've identified.
4. The list of users you're following is pictured here via their account thumbnail images (more about setting a thumbnail image a bit later in this chapter).

Next in the menu bar is the Profile link. This gives you a look at what others see when they navigate to your Twitter page via your user URL (http://twitter.com/mywayback in this case), as shown in Figure 3-10. At this time, my profile looks a bit bleak because I've only just begun this particular account and do not have many tweets to my name just yet.

Figure 3-10. You can see what other users see when you view your Twitter profile page.

When you click the Find People link from the navmenu, you'll gain access to the Twitter search function that allows you to seek out other users' Twitter accounts by entering the name of the person, business, or brand you are looking for in the Search field you see in Figure 3-11. If you click the Find Friends tab, you'll return to the screen that allows you to search for Twitter users that are listed as contacts in your Google, Yahoo, or AOL e-mail account. Invite by email allows you to enter valid e-mail addresses of people known to you so you can invite them to follow you on Twitter. Finally, the Browse Suggestions tab again returns you to the users of note that Twitter thinks you might enjoy following.

Figure 3-11. The Find People link allows you to search for folks to follow or invite others to follow you.

Moving along, click on Settings, the next text link from within the navmenu, and you'll gain access to the truly interesting aspects of your account, those that will allow you to further establish you, your brand, and your identity within the Twitterverse. While Twitter isn't as feature-rich as, say, a social networking site like MySpace, it still offers an appropriate amount of customization that is worth modifying. Begin with the Account tab within the Settings window (see Figure 3-12), and you'll see that you can modify your name, user name (yes, you can change it if you like), e-mail address, and time zone. You can also add a URL to another Web presence you manage, offer up a brief one-line bio, textually indicate your location, and also enable Geotagging to help third-party sites to annotate your geographic location via your device coordinates.

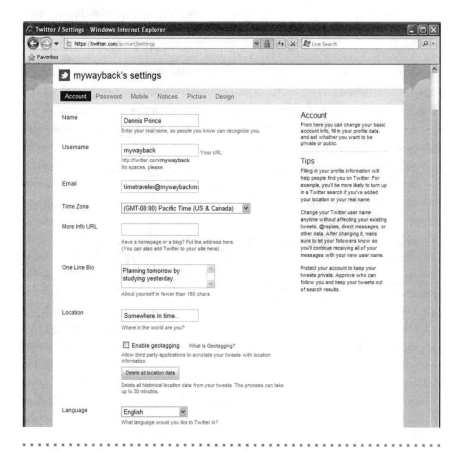

Figure 3-12. In the Account tab of the Settings screen, you can add more information about yourself and determine if you want your page and tweets visible to the public at large.

Of particular interest for those who wish to maintain a private Twitter presence and tweet only with a group of peers, coworkers, or close constituents is the check box near the bottom of the screen labeled "Protect my tweets." If you check this box, your tweets will be visible only to those you approve as followers—and no one else. It works like this: a user finds your account, navigates to your Twitter page, and is presented with a message that reads, "This person has protected their tweets." The user can then click the link labeled "Send request" to ask your permission to follow you. Once the user clicks this link, you'll receive a follower request that you must first approve before that user can begin receiving your tweets. If you ignore or flatly discard the request, the user won't receive your tweets. On the other hand, if you *do* want your tweets to be seen by the greater public without the need to approve follower requests, *don't* check this box. When you're satisfied with what you've entered in this screen, click the Save button.

Next, click the Password tab header within Settings to change your password. This is a good thing to do on a regular basis (about every six months or so) to ensure the integrity of your account security, especially if you think you account password has been inadvertently shared. Figure 3-13 shows how simple it is to change your password.

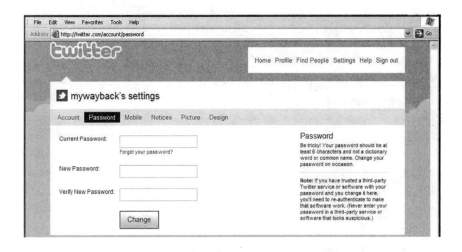

Figure 3-13. In the Password tab of the Settings screen, you can change your password quickly and easily.

The Mobile tab, located on the Settings screen, grants Twitter access to your mobile device setup, as previously illustrated in Figure 3-7. The Notices tab (see Figure 3-14) allows you to flag whether you want e-mail notification when you gain a new follower, when you receive a direct message, or when Twitter has some sort of news or update to share with the greater community. You can experiment with these flags to determine if you like receiving Twitter's automated messages or if they wind up adding only more clutter to your e-mail in-box.

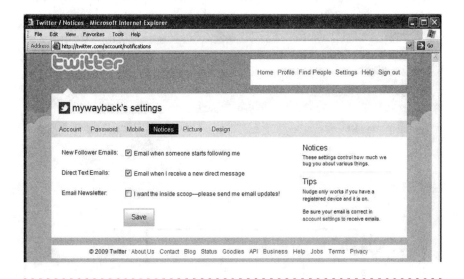

Figure 3-14. Still want more e-mail? Enable these flags for e-mail notifications.

Perhaps the most interesting settings for your Twitter page are those found within the Picture and Design tabs. As you can guess, the Picture tab allows you to upload an image, which will appear next to your user name in lieu of the default and nondescript bird silhouette icon that Twitter assigns you when you create your account. Uploading a new picture is easy, but you'll first need to find a suitable image. What's suitable? Basically, you're limited to an image that is about 139 pixels square, no larger than 700k, and in JPG, GIF, or PNG format. If you intend to use a close-up of your own smiling face, it will need to be quite a close shot in order for the community to get a good look at you. If you intend to utilize your brand logo or some other distinguishing element of your business as your image, be sure it is large enough to discern and is uncluttered by miniscule text that will be unreadable at this small size. When you have decided on a suitable image, simply use the Browse button within the Picture tab to locate the file from your local computer and then click the Save button. If the file is suitable, Twitter will update your image immediately (see Figure 3-15 for my before and after results).

Figure 3-15. Should you provide your own image for your Twitter account? Absolutely, as it will give a face to your online presence.

Last, click the Design tab within the Settings window to modify the color scheme and background image of your Twitter home page (see Figure 3-16). While you can choose from preestablished themes, those that will change your background, colors, and links, you can also select your own background image (check the Tile Background box, which appears after you click the Change Background Image button, if you intend a small image to be replicated for the complete background space). You can also manually change the colors of the different areas of the Twitter page as well as text colors by clicking on Change Design Colors. When you're satisfied with your modifications, simply click the Save Changes button to update your Twitter page design (or click Cancel if you believe you've made a real mess of things).

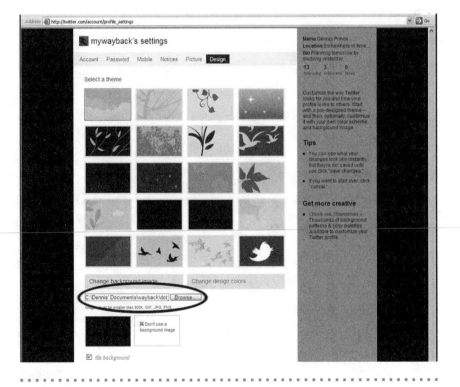

Figure 3-16. Modify the design of your Twitter page to avoid the doldrums of having a "default" existence within the Twitterverse.

So what are some tips regarding style and design for your Twitter page? Keep the design and style simple and relevant to your content. If you have a preexisting website design or company or brand logo, consider utilizing that (or at least the color scheme) within your Twitter design. Take some time to consider a user name and a style that fits your business and your intended voice and persona. Remember that you can make changes along the way, but try to consider your long-term goals and purpose at the outset. If you are constantly changing your Twitter presence, you likely will confuse your followers. Give it a good amount of thought, tie it back to your driving purpose, then get set up and get ready to interact.

4

Building Your Best Tweet

Now let's focus on the all-important tweet. It's the method of the messaging, but it requires a methodical approach if it's going to be useful, engaging, and effective. While you won't want to overthink your tweeting, you will want to be sure you have purpose in what you say, when you say it, and what you hope to achieve by doing so. This chapter digs deeper into the tweet and gives you yet more food for thought as you think about what you'll tweet and tweet about what you think.

■ ■ ■ Developing a 140-Character Sensibility

As I noted in Chapter 1, tweets are short microposts that consist of no more than 140 characters. While you may think that paring down your company's or product's message to so few letters, numbers, punctuation marks, and spaces is an impossible feat, take heart in the fact that hundreds of companies, both big and small, have mastered the art of the tweet.

Here are a few examples to get you started thinking about what your own message might be:

- From **CoffeeGroundz**: Open Mic night coming soon. It won't be a typical one either. Posting on the website will be soon. Every Thursday starting in Aug. (107 characters)
- From **LiveMusicBlog**: Latest: Photos: The Black Crowes @ Rothbury 2009: Here are photos from the Black Crowes set at Rothbury—http://bit.ly/vqKkL (108 characters)
- From **PlaidKidsCrafts**: *How is your summer crafting going so far? Send us a message!* (49 characters)

Now, while you may have thought you couldn't say much in twenty or thirty words, the three preceding tweets, all of which clearly communicate a specific, business-focused message in a concise and precise manner, should bolster your confidence. The fact is, because you're limited to 140 characters or less, you're able to say something quick and contained that is easy to read and digest by the message's recipients. Again, this is the anti—e-mail solution, the method of communicating without losing your audience's attention or interest. Sure, you'll need to consider your tweets ahead of time (usually), but when messaging to a customer base, why wouldn't you put thought into what you say before you say it?

It's not just the message recipients who benefit from the short messages; you benefit, too. Just think about how nice it will feel to be free from having to construct lengthy paragraphs or manual-length announcements. Instead, you consider what it is you want or need to say, and then you say it. Over time, you'll come to realize how much time and effort you save by using this method of concise communication. Of course, there is a downside to the short messaging; your tweets may sometimes become disjointed and even fragmented if you choose to message a larger thought stream over the course of successive tweets (remember the progressive freeway signs from Chapter 2?). Even so, with a bit of preplanning, you'll be able to manage your communications effectively and receive fast feedback from your followers about whether your message is having a positive impact.

■■■Keys for a Sweet Tweet

One of the best tweets I read on Twitter early on was as follows: *Write each word like it matters, because it does.*

Short. Simple. Relevant. That tweet spoke volumes in just 41 characters. To belabor the point would only dilute its impact and resonance. While it appears authoritarian, thanks to its directness and freedom from excuse or forgiveness, it fully embodies the author's personal view and reads as just that—a personal view. In this way, the tweet is succinct and presents itself as coming from a perspective of experience, yet it reveals itself as a belief of one member of the Twitter community. It's pure gold, though it likely wasn't labored over; the author just believed it and said it. When you craft your tweets, you should strive for the same elements. Of course, it's not necessary to establish a stunning statement each time you tweet, but you should try to include this essence in your messaging:

- Say what's on your mind, whether you are making a statement, asking a direct question, or pondering out loud and are open for input.
- Make it a useful, intriguing, or engaging message that would prompt your followers to respond, offer up answers, or even provide a contrary view for the purposes of establishing a healthy discussion.
- Keep it personable and indicative of your Twitter persona, be it business or personal.

Seems easy, doesn't it? If you're unsure about whether your tweets follow these guidelines, you'll want to step back a moment and revisit the key question I posed to you in Chapter 1: what is your reason for using the tool? Now, you don't have to go back and read Chapter 1 again, but if you do still wonder what you can achieve—what you *want* to achieve—using Twitter, you haven't yet defined your purpose and expectation of tweeting. Without this, you'll likely tweet in a rather scattered fashion, possibly bouncing from idea to idea without a sense of overall coherence. When this happens, your followers might stop reading because they've now wondered why it is they're bothering to read your messages. Even so, if you believe that you'll tweet about a multitude of topics and matters, perhaps you have yet to focus on how to leverage Twitter in a way that will mean the most to you and your business.

If you're looking to market a product or line of products, focus on that and speak to your readers about the value of the products while asking if they have any thoughts or experiences to share. If you're striving to establish a friendly voice for an existing business, then focus on engaging your readers in a way that's meaningful to them while avoiding constant sales pitches and solicitations of what it is that is of interest to your readers. After all, your friendly style will certainly work to draw folks in for a closer look at what you offer without your having to suggest it. Whatever your business purpose for tweeting—business networking, brand development, company image—be sure you are focused in your approach. When you are, the tweeting will roll off your fingers much easier than if you're not sure what you'll say next or why (see Figure 4-1).

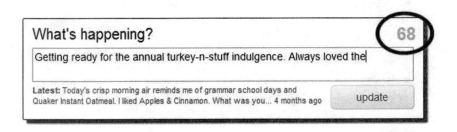

Figure 4-1. A tweet in progress: notice how the character counter (circled in the upper right-hand corner) indicates how many characters remain to be used.

Back to the content of the tweet itself, focus your thought and then express it within 140 characters or less. Some users will fire off random yet relevant messages, while others will plan a more thematic approach to their messaging. And at all times, successful tweeters will remain open to hot social, national, or global topics of the moment and will find a way to incorporate them into their messaging.

Sometimes a brief message that acknowledges a holiday, a notable event, or a development that affects a large segment of the population is enough to communicate that you *are* in touch and do care about what your followers care about. Then, after you tweet about the of-the-moment topic, you can move along to your original planned message stream, such as: *Today is Flag Day. What does this day means to you?* Then, later you might tweet: *Thanks for the feedback to yesterday's music survey. We're revamping our in-store playlist to include some of your suggestions. Visit our website for details.*

The follow-up tweet will probably prompt additional response and will keep the dialogue alive, your intention being to assure customers you've heard and valued their input. Later in the day, you can post another tweet that directs the discussion into the next topic you want to address with your customers. In a way, you can construct a messaging schedule—a daily checklist—of the sorts of tweets you'd like to broadcast. Consider these suggestions, exemplified by Starbucks's actual tweet stream:

- **Start of the day.** Begin with a message of salutation that acknowledges any notable event or news item that has transpired since your last tweet. For example: *This morning we had a total of 117 cars pay it forward in the @Starbucks drive thru by paying for the car behind them. Kindness at its best [9:15am].*

- **Midmorning.** Post a follow-up message to anything relevant or unfinished from the day before. In doing so, you will bring closure to a possibly still-open thread of discussion and display an element of continuity to your messaging. Now is possibly a good time to suggest the next topic to which you'd like to direct your readers' attention. Starbucks redirects its followers' attention like so: *We are* *hiring Baristas & Shift Supervisors. #Starbucks #Jobs. Please apply here: http://bit.ly/sWLlb (Feel free to RT) [10:59am].*

- **Lunchtime.** Time for midday break. Post a message that's light and relaxing about the morning that has just passed or the afternoon ahead. This is a social time, so be social and take the following tweet as an example of a good lunchtime update: *Proud to be a part of this. With @MorningJoe we're working to fix up the John McDonogh HS in New Orleans. See the video http://bit.ly/8PsSIR [11:55am].*

- **Afternoon.** Do you have any other action items on your tweet checklist? If so, post them now. Conversely, you could take the tack that Starbucks sometimes follows and offer up a fun question to your follower base: *If you could be a cup of coffee, what would you be? [2:59pm].*

- **Late afternoon.** Why not send a wrap-up message for those who followed you during the day that also serves as a shout-out to those who are just logging in, like Starbucks does in the following tweet? *Want to see how #StarbucksVIA stacks up against other instant coffees? The key part happens at 1:20 in the video: http://bit.ly/6fxtq9 [4:50pm].*

- **Evening.** If you're wrapping up your day, wish your readers a good evening or tell them the quick outcome of a previous discussion thread. Be sure to invite them for more discussion tomorrow. Or you could follow Starbucks's example and give them one last reason to visit your store before you close for the day: *Do you have a registered Starbucks Card? If so, you can get two hours of wifi per day: http://www.starbucks.com/card [6:50pm].*

Of course, you needn't follow this rigorous messaging schedule every day, but you should determine if your audience is receptive to regular communications like this. Also, you'll notice that you can maintain all-day interaction with just a handful of well-timed messages. You can tweet more if you like, but even at the rate just suggested, you'll demonstrate a perpetual presence while allowing your readers to chat among themselves, too.

As you construct your tweets, always remember to make your statements in concise sentences. (As shown in Figure 4-2, the counter will display a negative count of the excess characters if your tweet is too long.) Whenever possible, use proper grammar and short words to ease readers' understanding. Try to avoid excessive descriptors or overly emotional text that simply consumes characters. To both of these points, try to avoid the temptation of using excessive cyber-shorthand in your tweets. One tweet that I recently came across was, *I rd ur xclnt post*, which was meant to be interpreted as, *I read your excellent post*. The shorthand works here, but the intent of the statement is questionable. A more concise statement would have been *great post*, which makes it clear that the sender has read the post that was being referenced and thought it to be excellent—well, great, anyway. With the remaining 130 characters, the sender could complete his or her thought about the post just read.

Truthfully, if you find yourself using too much shorthand, you'll subject your readers to a game of "can you guess how that personalized license plate should read"? You get the idea; if you're having trouble making a coherent and compelling tweet within the 140-character limit, you might not yet have a grasp on what it is you really want to say. Follow other tweeters and see what you like and dislike about their messaging style, then practice a bit with your own. Most users confess

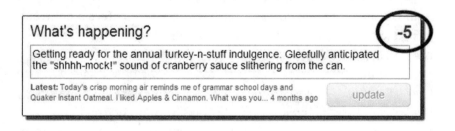

Figure 4-2. Oops! Too many characters in this tweet. Note the counter has begun displaying negative numbers. The Update button will be inactive until you bring the character count back down to 140 characters.

they're a bit clumsy with their tweets when they first start out, but they soon find a rhythm within a couple of weeks of regular use.

■ ■ ■ Giving Your Tweets a Voice

Having discussed matters of purpose and practice in the tweets you'll post, now it's time to consider the tone and style of your tweets. Most folks call this the "voice" of your tweeting, and it can make or break the success of what you have to say. Since the written word is subject to misinterpretation by many readers, you need to develop a style and mannerism that you will inject into your messages. For many companies and businesses, this voice often serves as the trademark of what they have to offer, and they work hard to establish, maintain, and protect it.

As you consider the voice you'll use for your tweets, you'll want to ask yourself a few questions:

- **Would your business, products, and services be benefited by a casual and free-spirited style, or would they be best served by an abrupt and matter-of-fact tone?** Only you can answer this question because only you know the "personality" of your business.

- **When you tweet, will you try to replicate the personality of your business, or will you establish a voice that offers a contrasting style?** For example, if you operate a law firm and your business personality is direct, factual, and legally technical, you might benefit from a Twitter voice that tries to boil your business down into layman's terms. Doing so will give those who are intimidated by the solid-oak-desk sensibility of the legal profession the impression that your firm is accessible to the masses and understanding of their needs.

- **Can the individuals whom you have selected to oversee your company's Twitter account maintain a consistent voice among themselves for your business?** Further, can they do so while avoiding the "drone" syndrome, wherein each tweeter always dutifully toes the company line and fails to fully engage your business's followers?

- **Is this a voice you'll be strapped to from this point onward?** If so, be sure to carefully consider your longest-term goals and ensure that the voice you adopt will suit and sustain that. If you are planning on evolving or reinventing your business, then you have more freedom to experiment with a voice that you can adapt to your followers' preferences.

To help develop the voice of your tweets, you'll want to consider how you'll message your readers. What you say will help to formulate how your readers perceive your voice, but your intention and your customers' perception will not always align. That said, consider how your messages can influence—or be influenced by—your intended voice:

- **Will you be in "tell" or "ask" mode in your messaging?** Depending upon your product or service, you'll want to decide if your customers want the reassurance of an authortarian voice (tell) or want open engagement of a communal and compassionate voice (ask). Of course, you can carefully mix both voice styles—and you should—as the need arises.
- **Will your messaging be all about you or all about your customers?** Believe it or not, some users become tagged as self-centered or even self-righteous if they're constantly talking about themselves or their business. If you must be in tell mode, consider softening your tone: *Did you know: We've gained favorable settlements for 97% of our clients, and we're proud of that. How can we help you?* Conversely, if you'll be in ask mode, ensure that you can maintain control of the conversation and be gracious—and thick-skinned—when you ask for candid feedback about you, your business, and your products. People are ready to tell you what they *really* think, so be ready for that.
- **Will you be able to hold your tongue while a discussion ensues?** If you start a discussion thread and the responses start pouring in, can you be patient enough to let your followers chat

among themselves without butting in? Some tweeters feel compelled to respond to nearly every response and in doing so unwittingly cut the conversation short. If this is you, then you're probably spending too much time monitoring for responses and too little time tending to other aspects of your business. More dangerous, if your followers detect constant responsiveness as your style, some might post messages simply to elicit a response from you, essentially baiting you for their own amusement. Make your statement, then let the rest of the forum talk for a while.

- **On the other hand, make sure you can be pleasantly conversational.** If you start a thought but don't follow up to provide closure for your followers, you might come off as aloof. A good practice is to ensure that you're available to message during the beginning and end of a thought thread, allowing your followers the lion's share of the middle of the discussion.

As you can see, voice will play a large role in how well you interact within the Twitterverse, and you'd be well advised to follow some other folks for a while to see how they make their voices heard.

■■■ Timing Your Tweets

A quick look back and you'll see we've discussed *why* to tweet, *what* to tweet, and *how* to tweet effectively. Now it's time to consider *when* to tweet. Even though the Internet is "always on," your target audience might not be. In fact, even though you're likely to establish an audience of followers who will drop in and out around the clock throughout the week, there are best times to tweet for maximum visibility and result. Look now at how timing plays an important role in your Twitter success.

Now, before you synchronize your watch to stand ready for the magic moment to broadcast your messages, be sure you've committed yourself to tweeting on a regular and reliable basis. In fact, just as the Internet thrives and survives based upon continual infusion of new content every hour of every day, so too does your Twitter result rely upon continual care and maintenance. Remember, you don't have to tweet all day long, but you should tweet every day to keep your followers interested and engaged. If you neglect posting, your followers might stop following and go look for someone else who offers a product or service similar to yours (yes, that would be your competitors). So, though we'll move on to determine the best time to broadcast your tweets, be sure you're prepared to keep the conversation flowing throughout the day and throughout the week, even to the point that you'll schedule "tweet reminders" in your daily calendar until you've developed a regular tweet habit.

So, what are the best times to broadcast your tweets? Well, the answer requires you to consider a couple of variables first:

- **Where is your core audience, that is, what time zone do they occupy?** Are they in the same zone as you, or have you amassed a following from across the continent or around the world? If you're truly global, and why wouldn't you want to be, then you'll need to make a judgment call on which audience to cater to when you tweet.
- **What is the local schedule of your intended core audience?** If you're on the West Coast of the United States, you might find you get best interaction when you post at 8:00 A.M., 12:00 P.M., and 5:00 P.M. Pacific time. Of course, your East Coast followers will be getting the message three hours later, so a message of *Good morning! Before your start your day, see our website for today's Good Morning Offer* that is posted at 8:00 A.M. Pacific time will be of diminished use to someone in New York City.

While you can't satisfy all time zones at all times, don't forget that the most useful tweet is a well-timed tweet. Again, if you wish to cater to followers who reside within a specific location—which is fine and acceptable—then indicate that intention within your brief Twitter bio notes. No matter how you serve the time zones, local or global, recognize the activity patterns of the audience you truly wish to engage and tweet in sync with its schedule to ensure your messages gain the maximum possible exposure every time.

The time of your tweets is important to consider, but you also will need to accommodate for the time *between* your tweets. As discussed earlier in this chapter, the matter of posting regularly but not too often is important to your results. Five tweets a day is plenty by the schedule suggested previously. Some think it's too many. Timing matters here because you need to allow enough time for followers to see your message and to respond if they feel so inclined. Also, patience on your part allows for cross-chatter to develop, giving you insight into your followers' thoughts, wants, and needs. Therefore, post the initial tweet and pause to allow for responses. Then, sum up the conversation (if needed) and move on to the next topic in your next tweet. It's important to keep the conversations on track and somewhat serial in flow (that is, one conversation or topic at a time) lest your Twitter log read like a sporadic outpouring of random thoughts and blurbs that will leave everyone—including you—confused.

Don't forget how important a role timing plays in your Twitter success. While you shouldn't become so rigid in your timing that you cut short some beneficial conversations, you should attempt to keep order and set expectations among your followers as to when they can expect to receive your next message.

▪▪▪ Every Tweet Has a Purpose

To round out our discussion of tweets, it's important to now revisit the matter of *why* to tweet. No doubt you're already planning and plotting your tweets, your eyes open to the depth behind those seemingly simple 140 characters. But before you look too far ahead at getting started in your tweeting, take one more look at the purpose of your tweets to make absolutely certain that you have a solid understanding of why you'll tweet and whether your intended messages will be greeted warmly or coolly by your potential followers.

First and foremost, you need to recognize that every tweet counts on Twitter. Because it's an open and, as of this writing, free-to-use platform, it's easy to digress into the aimless sort of yakking and yammering that causes many in the business world to brand Twitter as a high-tech henhouse of sorts. The challenge, then, is to consider every tweet you'll broadcast as if it has a price tag affixed to it. Really, consider how you'd use each message if you had to pay to transmit it, because the fact is that wasted or unwarranted tweets might resonate so poorly with your readers that they decide to "unfollow" you. In the business realm, a lost follower can be equated to a lost customer, who will no longer shop for your offerings. In a manner of speaking, then, a misplaced or otherwise misused tweet could cost you money in the end. Treat each tweet as if it has a cost (because each *does* have a value), and you'll be sure to make the most of every word in every message.

Next, be genuine in your tweeting. If your purpose is to grow your followers—again, your customer base—then you'll want to be honest and original in your tweeting. If you're struggling to sound sincere, your followers will detect it quickly. How can you maintain sincerity? Simply enough, ensure you're very clear about why you'll be using Twitter—that is, to reach out and candidly engage with your followers and customers—and when you faithfully offer direct access to you and your business, you'll be compelled to operate sincerely lest you lose your customers' trust and loyalty. Therefore, tweet what you know, what you feel, and what you believe. Ask yourself if you believe what you're tweeting and if you're truly interested in receiving responses and feedback. If the answer is yes, you can tweet comfortably and confidently toward your goals. If you're uncertain, you might need to continue refining your purpose in using Twitter for your business.

After you gain some comfort with tweeting, ask yourself if your messages are useful, compelling, and interesting. While you don't need to pound your followers with an unending litany of messages intended to coerce them all to sing the praises of your business or your brand, you should determine if your tweets offer your audience either information they can use or thoughts that might engage them in discussion. If you're not certain, you can even ask your followers, *Tell me if yesterday's post about [subject] was useful to you. Yes, or did you want to know more?* Trust me, they'll tell you, and you'll either gain the reassurance you needed or you'll find it's time to sharpen your message.

Of course, you don't necessarily need to ask a direct question to assess whether your messages are making an impact. A simple look at the number of responses your tweets receive, the "response ratio," can tell you if you're effecting the sort of dialogue and interaction you wanted or expected. Be patient in the early going, because you'll be finding your style while others will be finding you. If, after having established yourself on Twitter, you discover a sudden drop in your response ratio, something's gone astray in your overall messaging. Determine what it was and take steps to correct it. By all means, you also could discover that your followership and response ratio have suddenly spiked. Definitely figure out what prompted your sudden increase in popularity and do more of it (and bottle it, if you can).

In the end, if you're providing a value to the Twitterverse by way of your presence and messaging, the community will respond. The goal is to know what value you intend to offer your followers going in and be clear about what steps you will take to become a tweeter of interest, and maybe even impact. If this sounds lofty within the context of using Twitter in a business setting, consider how you felt the last time a business, service, or product made a positive impact on your life; you probably wanted to meet the person or people behind it, shake their hand, and thank them for the good experience. With Twitter, you literally have that opportunity at your fingertips. You decide what goal you want to achieve, what impact or influence you want to have, and then let these objectives guide you as you ready yourself for tweeting across the Twitterverse.

5

Sending Messages

NOW IT'S TIME TO start tweeting. In this chapter, you'll learn the different methods to send your messages—using the Web, a mobile device, or a third-party tool. You'll also learn how you can direct your tweets, that is, how you can post them for everyone's benefit, how to direct them to specific users, and even how to send private tweets without having to restrict your overall Twitter account from public viewing. Tweeting isn't difficult, that's for certain, and this chapter will help you get ahead of the learning curve from your very first day of tweeting.

■■■ Reviewing the Activity on Your Twitter Home Page

Upon logging into your Twitter account, you'll access your account home page where you can see the tweet activity of the folks you're following. For the sake of this example, I elected to follow a dozen of Twitter's suggested user accounts to demonstrate how your home page will be populated with tweets from users that interest you (see Figure 5-1).

Figure 5-1. When you log in to your Twitter account, your home page will display the tweets of those users you're actively following.

Note that your followers will not be able to see the tweets of those you follow if they navigate to your Twitter home page. Instead, they will be able to see only your tweet activity and the public responses your tweets generate. Click Profile to see what your followers see (Figure 5-2).

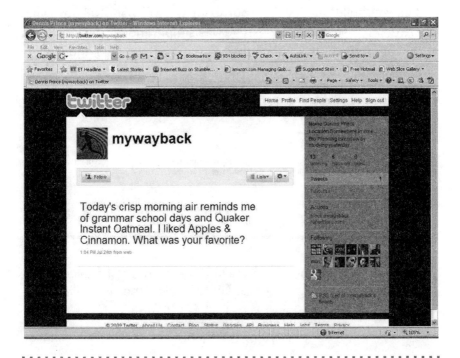

Figure 5-2. Ever wonder how your tweet stream is displayed in your followers' Web browsers? Take a look and see.

■■■ Sending Tweets

One day, as I took in the morning air, I was transported back to the days of my youth. Vivid memories of metal lunchboxes and oatmeal breakfasts filled my head, so I decided to tweet what was on my mind as of way of greeting and interacting with folks in the Twitterverse, and as you build a following, your followers will want to know what you're doing. Tweeting the message was simple enough, since located at the top of the Twitter home page is the message field and Update button to broadcast your tweet (see Figure 5-3).

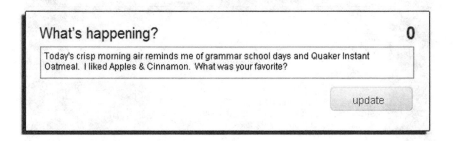

Figure 5-3.   Enter your tweet, watch the number of available characters to the right count down, then click the Update button to share your message.

That's it—in just a few seconds, I broadcast a message to the Twitterverse, my followers, and curious onlookers who might be following me soon (see Figure 5-4).

Figure 5-4. Image of your tweet on your home screen.

Notice the footnote below my posted update, which is visible from my home page (see Figure 5-5). It reads, "Less than one minute ago from web."

Figure 5-5. A footnote below each tweet will time-stamp it and provide information about how it was sent.

This time stamp indicates to my readers, and to me, how recent the message is and what method was used to post it ("web"). Look at tweets from other users to monitor how often they're posting and what method they're using to do so. One note of caution about the tweets you post: once you've posted them, you can't edit them. As of this writing, Twitter does not allow users to edit their updates, so be confident that your tweets adequately relay your intended messages before you publish them. If you absolutely make a mess of a message, you can delete the update entirely by clicking the tiny trashcan icon, which is visible only to you from your home page (see Figure 5-6).

mywayback Today's crisp morning air reminds me of grammar school days and Quaker Instant Oatmeal. I liked Apples & Cinnamon. What was your favorite?
about 3 hours ago from web · Delete

Figure 5-6. If you're dissatisfied with one of your tweets, you can't edit it, but you can use the Delete icon to delete it.

The previous update is an example of a "public message," one that everyone can see if they follow me on Twitter or happen to find my page. The message was intended to be seen and hopefully commented on by anyone who might find it interesting. Sometimes, however, you'll see tweets that include an extra notation, *@username* (see Figure 5-7). These tweets are "replies" and are intended as a response for the user whose name was specified after the "at" symbol.

I could go for some warm edamame RT @NegativeNatalie: Its 100 degrees. But I want won ton soup. Um that's not normal
about 20 hours ago from TweetGenius

Figure 5-7. When you see the *@username* notation, it indicates the tweet was intended as a response to a specific user.

The reply feature allows a tweeter to engage with his or her followers by answering questions or otherwise partaking in brief dialogue that is specific to that user. Keep in mind that your replies are visible to the public, but don't let this discourage you from using this method to respond to other Twitter users! Replying is a good practice, since it shows you're actively reviewing your home page activity and are interested enough to engage your followers. Twitter has made replying even easier by adding a reply icon—a back-pointing arrow—that tweet recipients can see when they hover their mouse pointer over a tweet, then click to automatically initiate a reply with the @*username* information pre-populated to the reply (see Figure 5-8). As an added benefit, whenever an active user's user name is specified in a tweet, that user-name notation becomes an active link to the user's Twitter home page. In this way, if people reading the reply are interested in the user's original question, they could navigate to that user's Twitter page and engage that user directly or begin following that user. For this reason, it's a good idea to find appropriate users to follow and message with, because doing so increases your visibility to others who might not have found you yet.

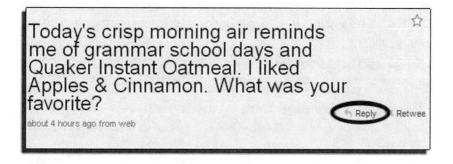

Figure 5-8. This "reply" arrow makes it easy to reply to received tweets.

There will be times when you want to respond to a specific user but do not want the public to see your reply. Without having to disable your account from public view, you can use the *direct message* feature of Twitter to send a private reply to another Twitter user (see Figure 5-9). To do this, simply include the direct message command in front of your reply, *D + username + message*, as in: *D mywayback I always preferred Cream of Wheat...yummy.*

The direct message will be delivered only to the user indicated and will not be displayed in the public viewing area of your home

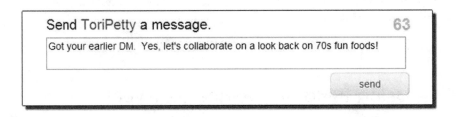

Figure 5-9. Direct messages can be sent only to those who follow you, and they won't be displayed in your public tweet stream.

page or in that of the user you direct-messaged. Again, this is a way to manage momentary private exchanges without disabling your entire account from public view.

And what if you want to regain the visibility of one of your previous tweets or you loved a public tweet from someone else and would like to forward it to your followers? All you need do is *retweet*. There's no special functionality to retweeting; when at your Twitter home page, simply run the mouse over the lower right-hand corner of the box with the message you want to retweet, and click on the Retweet button that appears. If you retweet a message you previously had transmitted in order to increase its visibility again, users who see it will immediately recognize it as a retweet because of the RT notation. And if you want to forward along a tweet you received from someone you're following, add the RT notation to the message to indicate that you are forwarding another user's message to your followers (see Figure 5-10). And, adjacent to the reply arrow when you mouse over a tweet, you'll find the retweet arrow and text link on a tweet.

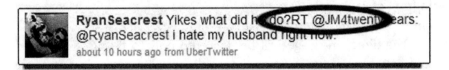

Figure 5-10. Look for the RT notation in a tweet, which indicates that it's a *retweeted* message.

■■■Using a Mobile Device to Tweet

Probably the biggest contributor to Twitter's sharp and sudden rise in popularity is how it lends itself to mobile device usage. Clearly, to answer "what's happening?" for your audience of followers, you need to be able to answer any time, anywhere, and the mobile messaging functionality of Twitter allows that. If you need to revisit how to set up your mobile device for Twitter, go back to Chapter 3 to see how quick and easy it can be.

Tweeting from a mobile device is just like messaging from the website, with the exception that you'll need to send your text message to the Twitter "short code." What's that? In simple terms, a short code acts like a standard phone number, except it's shorter (naturally) and used for the purpose of transmitting text-based messages. You don't need a particular type of phone to perform this task; any phone that supports text messaging (most do these days) along with a phone service that supports texting will do. Twitter doesn't charge you for receiving and posting and distributing mobile-based tweets, but your mobile service provider will charge you each time you send or receive a single message—unless you have a text-messaging plan, which provides you with an allotted number of texts (or unlimited texts from some providers) per month for a flat fee. (Check with your provider before you start tweeting from your mobile device.)

To send a tweet from your mobile device, simply create your text message (140 characters, remember) and send it to the 40404 short-code (if you're in the United States). It's that simple, and Twitter will ensure it gets posted to your home page and is made available to your followers. The complete list of global Twitter short codes is as follows:

Short codes for two-way Twitter SMS:
- United States: 40404
- Australia: 0198089488 (Telstra customers)
- Canada: 21212
- India: 53000 (Bharti Airtel customers)
- Indonesia: 89887 (AXIS and 3 customers)
- Ireland: 51210 (O2 customers)
- New Zealand: 8987 (Vodafone and Telecom NZ customers)
- UK: 86444 (Vodafone, Orange, 3 and O2 customers):

One-way long codes:
- Germany: +49 17 6888 50505
- Sweden: +46 737 494222
- All other countries: +44 762 4801423

To stay updated on the latest list of Twitter short codes, visit the Twitter Phone FAQ online at http://help.twitter.com/forums/10711/entries/14014.

Back to the messaging itself, you can send any kind of update to users you specify with your mobile phone, including retweets, direct messages, and replies. Simply enter the same command prompts into your tweet text that you would into Twitter's message field for the type of update you wish to send. Similarly, if you have enabled your mobile device to receive messages and updates (refer to Chapter 3, Figure 3-5) from those you follow, their tweets will be sent to and be viewable from your mobile device as text messages. As a cautionary bit of advice, because you're enabled to tweet from your mobile device, anywhere and any time, don't forget to consider the timing of your updates, allowing others plenty of time to respond, as discussed in Chapter 4. Otherwise, if you're on the go and need to tweet, by all means do so.

■ ■ ■ Enlisting a Third-Party Tool for Tweeting

Historically, whenever a new Web- or computer-based tool surfaces and gains favor and popularity, companies and individuals scurry to create add-on tools and tweaks intended to improve users' experience of the application. Twitter is no different, and many independent third-party tool developers, that is, application designers and marketers not associated directly with Twitter, have stepped forward to add more features to the tweet toolset.

Often, these third-party developers solve problems or address shortcomings with an original application, incorporating fixes or enhancements into their tools that the originating company hasn't had the opportunity to address directly itself. Sometimes these add-on tools provide an extra layer of fluff that isn't truly needed at the end of the day. And sometimes these tools simply mimic the methods of an existing suite of computer tools in a way that some users prefer over what the originating company has developed. When it comes to Twitter, there are many such add-ons and extensions to what the company has already provided. Whether the core functionality of Twitter is suitable to you is a question only you can answer. However, if you're curious about some of the most popular third-party toolsets, consider these three front-running applications.

■ ■ TWHIRL (HTTP://TWHIRL.ORG)

Hands down, this PC-based tool is the most talked about as of this writing. The Twhirl tool offers access to your Twitter account and activity without the need to launch a Web browser application (see Figure 5-11). Once you've downloaded the application (it's free to download and use), you can keep track of your Twitter account, send and receive tweets, and search the sea of tweets crossing the Twitterverse. It's designed to run on both PC and Mac operating systems but requires you install the Adobe AIR application first. Naturally, Twhirl has a Twitter presence that you can follow at http://twitter.com/twhirl.

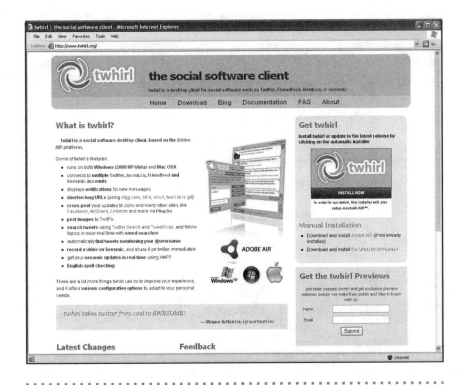

Figure 5-11. One of the most oft-mentioned third-party Twitter tools is Twhirl.

▪ ▪ TwInBox (http://techhit.com/twinbox)

Formerly known as OutTwit, this application allows you to manage your Twitter activity *within* the Microsoft Outlook e-mail application. This integration makes TwInBox truly useful since Outlook users often keep the e-mail application up and running constantly, or at least, very frequently. Integration of Twitter access within Outlook (sending and receiving tweets) allows you to manage all of your messaging from a single application window. Oh, this one's free to download and use, too (see Figure 5-12).

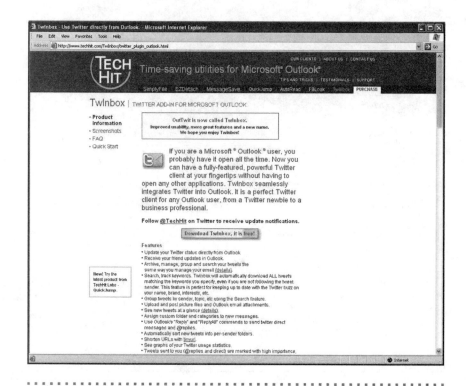

Figure 5-12. For Microsoft Outlook users, TwInBox allows you to send and receive tweets within the e-mail application.

▪ ▪ TWITTERRIFIC (HTTP://TWITTERRIFIC.COM)

This application is intended solely for the Mac audience and does require purchase (a mere $14.95). The purpose of this tool, which also allows access to the usual Twitter activity and interaction, is to minimize the Twitter view into a tiny desktop window that allows the Mac user visibility of the tool without cluttering a likely already-busy workspace (see Figure 5-13).

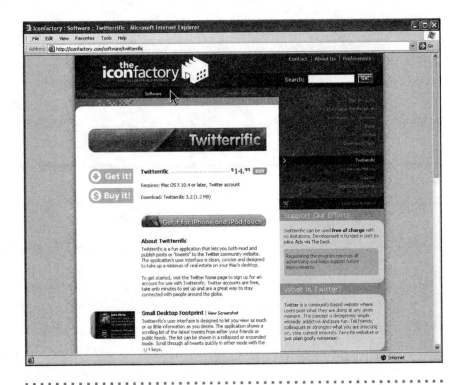

Figure 5-13. For Mac users, Twitterrific appears to be the third-party tool of choice.

Before you try using a third-party tool like these or any others you'll encounter, get comfortable with tweeting back and forth via the Twitter site, Web-based or mobile, to see how it works for you. (Visit the Twitter Wiki Apps page for an up-to-date listing at http://twitter. pbworks.com/Apps.) Start your tweeting today and develop a rhythm to your communication. You'll soon get into a groove of tweeting and will be able to further hone your approach in your use of Twitter for your business, brand, or other such endeavor.

6

Searching and Following

Now that you're actively tweeting, you might feel a little self-conscious if you're not receiving any responses to your updates. Actually, the start-up is somewhat difficult for all users, but don't let this cause you to immediately question your original intent; you've just begun, and it will take a bit of time for others to notice you've arrived. In this chapter, we'll look at how to find other users and how they might find you. Then, we'll look at what it means to follow another tweeter, how becoming a follower yourself can gain followers to your tweets, and how all of this can boost how effective you are at reaching your target audience.

The Lead-In About Following

What does it mean to follow someone on Twitter? Well, do you recall when you created your Twitter account and were provided with a list of suggested users you could begin following immediately? If you chose to follow any one of these individuals, then you know that *following* is

Twitter-speak for receiving a user's status updates. If you think about it, you'll come to the conclusion that "following" actually is what Twitter is all about. If you're not following anyone on Twitter, then you're not gaining anything from this tool. What's more, as you'll learn later on in this chapter, if you decline to follow any of your fellow Twitter users, it is doubtful that you will gain a real following yourself. Without following or followers, you might as well write your tweet-able thoughts on scraps of paper and stuff them into a desk drawer.

So, whom should you follow? To answer that question, you'll want to discover who is out there to follow. When you find other users that interest you or share interests similar to yours, you should follow them and begin replying to some of their tweets when you feel you have something to contribute to the topic of the moment. When you contribute to the discussion, you make yourself visible to those users as well as to those users' audiences of followers. A user might engage you directly in response, or the user's followers might likewise comment to your tweet. This is how the conversation gets rolling and how you can begin to include yourself in the discussion at hand. Remember that when you tweet in response to someone you're following, your Twitter user name becomes visible and provides an active link to your Twitter page. When others find your responses to be of interest, they might decide to link back to your Twitter page and begin following you.

If this all sounds like a vintage primer in how to break the ice at a cocktail party, it is. With a beverage in hand and a smile on your face, you wander up to a conversation that is already underway, listen for a moment, then determine if there's something of interest or value you can add to the discussion. When you do, others notice you and begin to engage you. You wouldn't presume to dominate the discussion. Instead, you just add your input as appropriate. If others take an interest in you, they might follow you to the snack table and pursue a deeper discussion with you based on your comments in the previous group chat. To this end, it's important your initial comments be relevant and useful, lest you look like a party crasher. If you think it sounds like fun, it is. Now, let's find a conversation for you to join in on.

■■■ Simple Searching for Someone to Follow

To see what other interesting conversations are underway in the Twitterverse, you'll want to begin with a search. Thankfully, Twitter has made it easy to search other conversations, by topic or by user name (or company or brand name). For starters, log in to your Twitter account. You will immediately be directed to your home page, where you'll find several methods to search for other users. See Figure 6-1 for these search options:

The Find People link in the navigation menu allows you to search for other users by way of matching their user name, first name, or last name.

The Search field allows you to enter any keyword to search for related tweets that have recently been posted. Since it's a free-form search, you might match on a topic word, a user name, a company or product name, and so on.

The Trending: Worldwide area includes one-click links to tweets relevant to the topics noted. These are the most tweeted topics of the moment, and they might present a good opportunity for you to weigh in on the latest buzz.

Figure 6-1. From your Twitter home page, there are several immediate options for searching out other users or topic tweets.

For the sake of this example, I clicked on the "Harry Potter" link under the Trending Topics area and gained a list of matching tweets, as seen in Figure 6-2. Take special note that Twitter also informed me that additional matching entries had been found since the time of my search and gave me the option of refreshing the display of matches. Additionally, see the Save This Search button that allows you to store this search in your profile so you can check it periodically to locate more users of interest. Use the search function for a day or two and scour the Twitterverse for people and items of interest.

Figure 6-2. A list of matching tweets will be displayed after you've initiated your search.

Once you've found someone you want to follow, all you need do is visit the user's Twitter page and click the Follow button, which is located beneath the user's profile picture (see Figure 6-3). If that user's Twitter updates are not protected, you will immediately begin receiving his or her update stream, which will be visible from your home page. Conversely, if the user has protected his or her updates, you'll need to have that user approve you as a follower before you can begin receiving his or her updates.

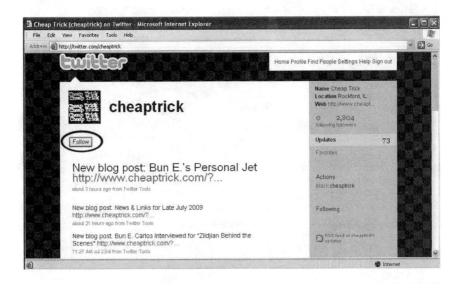

Figure 6-3. I chose to follow a band that always takes me way back and keeps me current, too.

If you're using Twitter from a mobile device, you can still follow users by texting the following command to the Twitter short code: *follow username.* So, had I been using my mobile device when I chose to follow user cheaptrick, I would have texted the following: *follow cheaptrick.* And what if you want to stop following someone? All you need do is click the gear icon dropdown menu, and then click the Unfollow section (see Figure 6-4). From a mobile device, you can stop following a user by texting *leave username* to the Twitter short code.

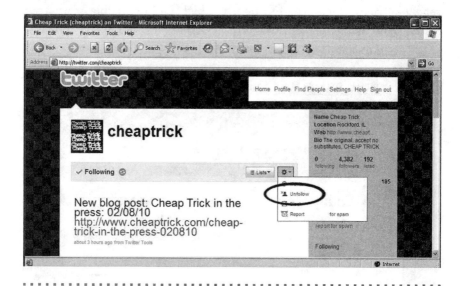

Figure 6-4. To stop receiving updates from a user, click Unfollow on the user's Twitter home page.

■ ■ ■ Advanced Searches Within Twitter

If the "simple search" that I just described doesn't suit you, there is a more advanced method of seeking out and sifting through the Twitter activity. From any browser window, type in the URL address http://search.twitter.com. This is Twitter's official search page (see Figure 6-5). Notice this page has a search field that operates identically to

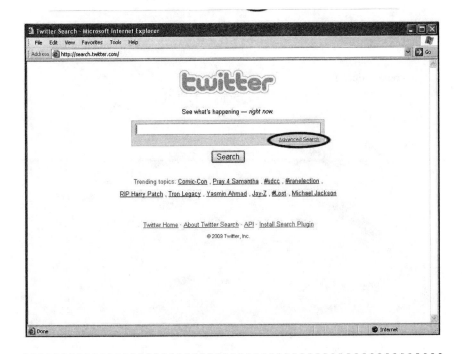

Figure 6-5. Use the Advanced Search below the Search field at http://search.twitter.com to access more search functionality.

the one you found on your Twitter home page, as shown previously in Figure 6-1. Look a little closer, however, and you will see the text link for Advanced Search just below the search field; click that, and you'll navigate to Twitter's Advanced Search screen (see Figure 6-6), where you can truly narrow your search to locate precisely who or what you hope to find within the Twitterverse.

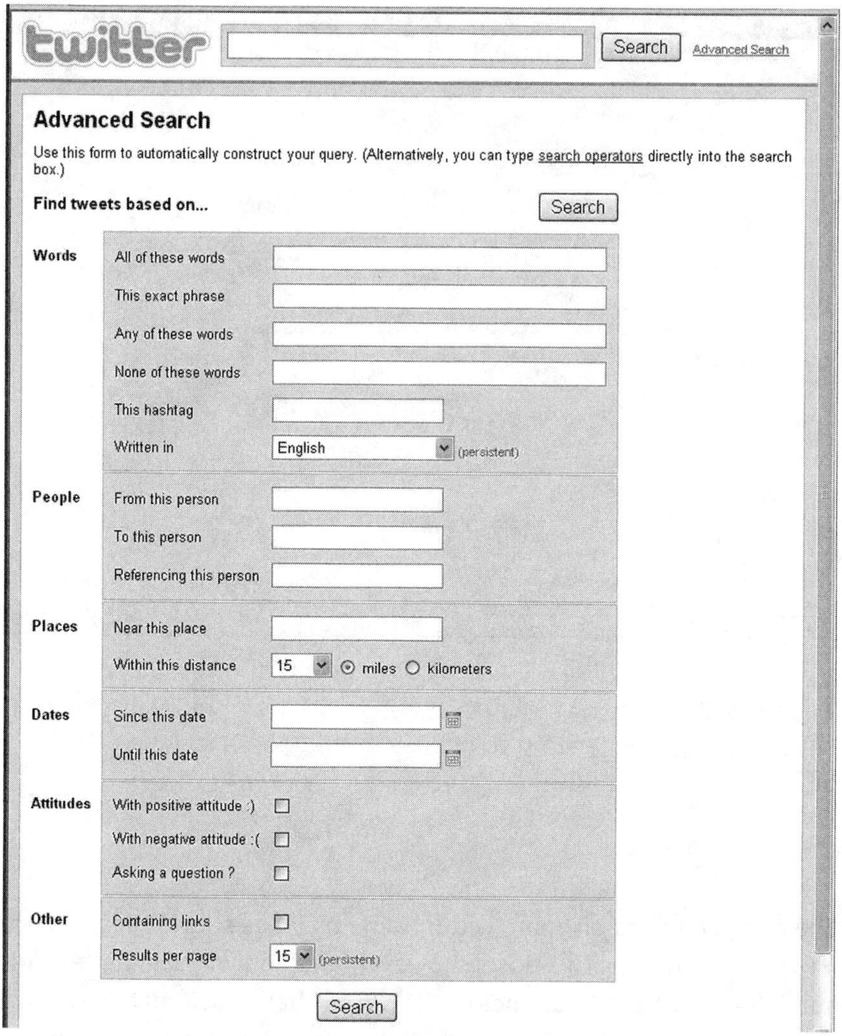

Figure 6-6. The Advanced Search screen allows you to truly hone in on exactly who or what you're looking for.

Further, you can also utilize Twitter's defined *search operators*, or commands that will help you refine your searches, to do an advanced search from within the regular Search field. Here's a list of commands you can use in your advanced searching:

Search Operator	_To Find . . ._
Twitter search	This is the default free-form operator that will search for the words you specify (such as "Twitter search"), regardless of where or when they appear in matching tweets.
"happy hour"	Use opening and closing quotation marks to find tweets containing an exact phrase, such as "happy hour."
love **OR** hate	Use the "or" operator to find tweets that contain one or more search terms you specify. The example here will result in matching tweets containing either "love" or "hate" (or both).
beer−root	Use the minus-sign ("−") operator to find tweets that contain one word but not another. This operator is useful when some search terms are associated with multiple other words that you wish to filter from your search results. The example here will result in matching tweets containing "beer" but not "root."
from:username	Use the "from:" command to search for updates sent from a specified user name.
to:username	Use the "to:" command to search for updates sent to a specified user name.
@username	Use the "@" command to search for updates that reference a specified user name.
"happy hour" **near:** "san francisco"	Use the "near:" command to search for updates containing a specified topic or words that were sent from a location that is in close proximity to the one specified (based upon the location in send users' account specifications).

| superhero **since:** 2010-03-01 | Use the "since:" command to identify a time stamp for your search, which will produce search results that contain specified words or terms that have been posted since the indicated date (in YYYY-MM-DD format). |
| ftw **until:**2010-03-01 | Use the "until:" command to establish an end date for updates you're searching for. All search results will have been posted before the date specified (in YYYY-MM-DD format). |

To wrap up this discussion of finding users whom you might want to follow, you can also refer to an interesting tool on the Web that provides a complete directory of Twitter users, culled and collated for you. Visit TwitDir.com to access the online Twitter directory (see Figure 6-7). At that site, you'll see a listing of the most active and prolific tweeters, some of whom you may wish to follow.

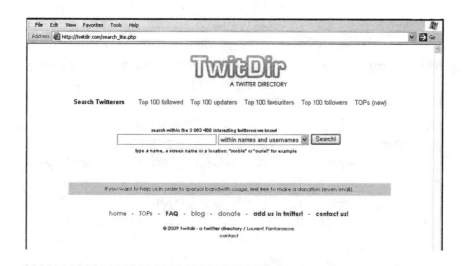

Figure 6-7. Visit TwitDir.com for the who's who in the Twitterverse.

■ ■ ■ Why Someone Would—or Wouldn't— Want to Follow You

Now that you understand how to search for and follow other users, it's time to ask yourself a hard question: "*Would* someone want to follow me?" Well, if you have interesting information to share with others about yourself and your business, product, or service, then you're well on your way to attracting followers who share a want or need for what you have to offer. There are, however, other elements about your overall Twitter presence and style that could make or break your ability to attract and retain followers. Consider these elements as you "dress" for success at Twitter:

- **Do you have a profile photo or image?** If you're using the default image that Twitter assigned you when you created your account, you'll seem lazy, unaware, or possibly not even real. Users might find themselves wondering if some bot created your account. Make sure you establish a profile photo or image immediately upon the creation of your account.
- **Does your Twitter user name match your profile photo and the overall tone of your business or product?** If you have a strange profile picture, an odd (or even unfriendly or unseemly) user name, or your tweets don't seem aligned with the image your Twitter profile portrays of you, you'll likely struggle to attract the kind of followers that would otherwise be interested in learning more about you and your business.
- **If you've borrowed an identifiable photo or image that *isn't* you, well, that's just odd and would even be considered spammy, a weak attempt to attract followers by "pimping" someone else's well-known face or brand.** Put your best face forward, literally, in order to fully and honestly connect with your followers. "Posers" typically aren't appreciated within the Twitter community and, as a business, to pretend to be anyone or anything else than what you truly are would be detrimental to properly representing your brand, product, or service.

- **Do you tweet regularly?** If you have a great page with a name that promises great information or compelling updates but do not maintain a regular stream of tweets, then folks will wonder if the account is still being maintained.
- **Are your tweets interesting, appropriate to your purpose, and respectful of the community?** If you're perpetually just making blunt sales pitches or posting the same message or pitch day after day, then you're offering nothing of interest to the Twitterverse that would attract followers.
- **When you tweet, do you tweet about other users or topics, not just about you or your business?** If your tweets are always about you, you'll struggle to establish the sort of inclusive conversations that show you're deeper than your business, brand, or product.
- **Are you actively following users that follow you?** There's a mutuality about Twitter, and folks who follow you typically appreciate the reciprocal follow from you. You don't need to follow everyone that follows you (in fact, you'll read in a moment why this isn't a good approach), but you should strive to interact with your followers and keep abreast of their updates.

Consider the foregoing elements when you're looking to build a following and recognize that, like anywhere else, the way you present and conduct yourself on Twitter will directly impact how well you can build an audience that is interested to learn more about you and your business.

■■■ Mining for Mass Following?

There is a disagreement among Twitter users, especially among those who are in pursuit of the business benefits that the social networking tool offers. Many call Twitter a "numbers game" and insist that the goal is to attract as many followers as possible so as to indicate your value within the Twitterverse. After all, if hordes of people are following you, you must be worthwhile, right? To be sure, the more folks you can virtually shake hands with, the better your chances for reaching more potential customers or clients, and to a degree, this approach works. By the same token, however, since Twitter is so easy for anyone to access and use, it is doubtful that the potential quality of the Twitter masses is very high. Put another way, you might be gaining a legion of followers, but how many of them might truly be customers or clients? Perhaps these folks are mass-following anyone and everyone who shows up on Twitter as a way for them to increase their own follower count. So while it makes good sense for you to follow a reasonable volume of folks in order to develop some beneficial relationships, business or personal, you'll need to ensure that those who follow you are really interested in what you have to say or offer.

You don't only have to gain Twitter followers; you also have to manage your Twitter followers (just as some will manage you as their follower). Within a few hours of having created the mywayback account at Twitter, I received notification that several users had begun following me. I was delighted, of course, that these users had already found me and decided my premise was interesting enough to follow, but then I read their tweet streams. The content of their tweets led me to deduce that these users essentially were just eager to build a following of their own by following as many users as possible. Frankly, they didn't have much to contribute to my intent, nor would they likely be interested in my tweet stream. In the end, I decided that they were probably useless followers to me and blocked them from my tweets. Yes, that sounds harsh, but that is the reality of Twitter, and for anyone interested in maximizing the monetization potential of Twitter, it's important to develop a following that's truly suitable to your purpose. If you're struggling with this approach, consider an example in which you own a bookstore and several customers show up only to read in your store and drink your free coffee but never make a purchase. Get the idea?

If you still think this approach is a bit too aggressive, take a look at one of the users following my account. Take note of the content of this user's updates, and then look at this user's ratio of "following" to "followers" (see Figure 6-8).

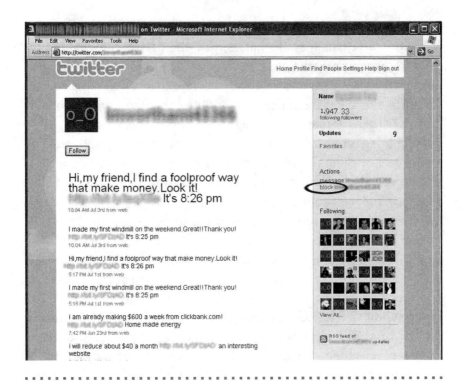

Figure 6-8. Clearly, this is not a high-value follower, so I'll block this user from cluttering my followers list.

From Figure 6-8, notice this user (whose name has been obscured for anonymity) is following 1,947 other users but only has 33 followers of his own. He has updated his tweet stream only nine times in total, and each of the nine tweets seems to be a hard-pitch post that hasn't garnered a single reply. This user seems to be attempting to play the mass-followers numbers game, so I'm going to remove him from my followers list by clicking the Block text link you see circled in Figure 6-8. This will remove him from my followers list. Now I can continue focusing on followers who might be of greater interest to me and my pursuits and offer value to their stream of updates.

You're now ready to begin searching for folks to follow, and maybe you will even gain their following as well. Be sincere in whom you choose to follow, just as you hope others will be sincere in their following of you. This is the beginning of the engagement process that is afforded to you when you use Twitter. Further, this is also the start of the incredible business networking potential that awaits you, which is a topic that will be discussed in more detail in Chapter 9.

7

Keeping the Tweet on Key

BY NOW YOU HAVE already begun tweeting and establishing your presence and persona within the Twitterverse. If you have been tweeting for a few weeks and still haven't gathered the number of followers you had hoped to gain by this point in time, don't change course! Sure, the Twitter start-up period can seem a bit lonely at first, but that's no reason for you to abandon your original, well-thought-out purpose and approach to tweeting. So, again, I urge you to resist the temptation at this critical moment to suddenly change your tactic and alter your message in order to gain attention, as doing so will cause your tweets to stray off course and off key. Trust me: if you have fully considered and planned out your Twitter presence, then it is only a matter of time before other Twitterers begin gravitating to what you're tweeting about. In this chapter, then, you'll find more tips, tactics, and guidance to ensure your tweets keep to your core purpose and principle for using Twitter.

■ ■ ■ Back to the Egg

Before diving deep into the nuances of your ongoing tweet stream, pause a moment and ask yourself, am I still on track with my original Twitter intent, or would it make sense to refine my tweet recipe at this stage in the game? During your start-up period, you should keep pulse of the following:

- **Are your tweets timely?** To this point, ask yourself not only if you are regularly posting updates to your tweet stream but also whether the content of your tweets is relevant to what's going on in both your business and the world itself. If you are offering your followers a special seasonal deal, for instance, are you tweeting about that discount with enough advance notice for your followers to take advantage of it before it expires? On the more conversational side of the Twitter equation, it is equally important that you engage in non-business updates that acknowledge current events. Doing so lets your followers know you're in touch with larger global issues and are not only interested in jamming sales pitches down their virtual throats at all times.

- **Are you actively reading the tweets of others?** While you don't want to lapse into copycat messaging, you should keep tabs on those you follow to see what they're tweeting about, as well as what sort of responses those tweets are getting. Staying up-to-date on what others are talking about can help you keep track of what trends the Twitterverse is abuzz about at any given time. Additionally, peek into the hot topics of discussion that are regularly posted on Twitter's main page (see Figure 7-1).

- **Are you still driving the discussion without driving away your followers?** It's your tweet stream, so you should maintain control over where it goes and when it goes there. Remember to allow your followers to respond to your posts, and from time to time you can even let them post a response to your tweet stream that's somewhat off-topic if you think their tweet will benefit your followers in some way. While you should eventually pull the discus-

Figure 7-1. The Twitter home page features hot topics of discussion that will keep you abreast of the recent buzz-worthy chatter.

sion back to your purpose, make sure you're not doing so in a way that offends a faithful follower.

Now, let's circle back and determine how well you're managing the construction and consistency of your tweets. Analyze your tweeting activity to determine if your tweets adhere to the following guidelines. Is there anything else can do to improve your messaging?

- **Keep it short.** Sure, because you only have 140 characters to work with, you have no option but to be brief with your tweets. However, consider squeezing your message into an even smaller character count. If you're posting an update to inform your followers of something new or special you're offering, use the tweet to quickly explain your offer and then embed a condensed URL that your followers can immediately click on to obtain more relevant information (see Figure 7-2).
- **Keep it readable.** While it certainly makes sense to squeeze and squish letters into some sort of intelligible string of abbreviations, the fact is that doing so too often will render your messages confusing or even annoying to your target audience. Unless you're

seeking a following of thirteen-year-olds in hopes of gaining a new BFF, unbridled use of social messaging shortcuts could result in a TTYL from your best followers.

- **Keep it relevant.** If I've said it once, I'll say it again: remember your purpose for tweeting and keep your updates relevant not only

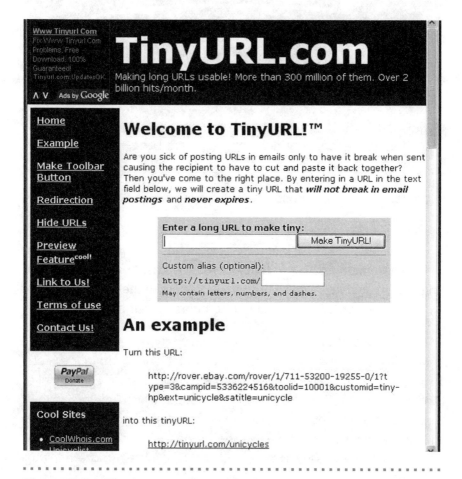

Figure 7-2. The best tweeters use TinyURL's service at http://tinyurl.com to condense long Web-page addresses into compressed, mini versions of themselves. TinyURLs will direct your followers exactly where you want them to go and are perfect for a short but effective tweet!

to that objective but also to the daily and weekly rhythm your followers have come to expect and enjoy from you.

■ **Keep it coming.** Yes, even when it seems like there's nobody listening, keep tweeting. If you stop updating, your followers will stop listening. What other choice would they have?

Maximizing your use of and efficiency with Twitter is like any discipline in that it requires that you continually recheck and revise your activity, your intent, and your style. Keep your sights to the future but be sure to keep an objective eye on your tweeting to ensure you're getting the most out of your effort.

■ ■ ■ Tweeting for Improved Presentation

There's a side benefit to tweeting that many Twitter users routinely overlook, despite the fact that they're forced to embrace it with every tweet they send out into the Twitterverse: the development of concise and compelling communication skills. When it comes to business outreach, wherein marketers and salespeople have a tiny window of opportunity to capture their audience's attention, concise communication is essential and forms the cornerstone for business success. The same holds true when it comes to successfully engaging users on Twitter. With so much information blurring the Internet skies, you need to say your piece quickly in a way that makes your followers slow down for a few moments to consider what you've just stated. To that end, the following is a list of recommendations that will help you tweet on key and in brief but engaging bursts:

■ **Treat each tweet as if it were a news story headline.** Review recent headlines that caused you to pause and read further into the full article. Ask yourself what it was about the construction or the content of the headline that caught your attention.

■ **Compose your tweets in a way that has your followers begging for more.** When you're brief but captivating, your followers will be grabbed by what you've said and will want to know more.

Make sure to include a TinyURL link that will direct your followers to more information on the topic you've just tweeted so they can dig deeper.

- **Don't overstay your welcome on your followers' Twitter feeds with a rambling update.** Say what you have to say, and if your followers want to learn more, make it easy for them to do so. This way, if they're not particularly interested in a certain update of yours, you haven't taken much of their time with a topic or idea that holds little interest or relevance to them at that moment.

- **Be especially attentive to feedback and responses that indicate that one of your previous tweets was ambiguous or otherwise unclear.** Use that feedback immediately to sharpen your next transmission of communication.

- **Choose your words carefully, since the typewritten word cannot be clarified through the use of tonal inflections or nuances.** All too often, Twitter users unintentionally offend or otherwise alienate one of their followers by what they write in their tweets, even though they don't intend to do so. If you're hearing implied inflection inside your head as you construct a tweet, remember that your followers *won't* hear it. If it could be misconstrued, rewrite the update to keep your messaging clear.

The easiest way to construct a better and briefer tweet is to put yourself in your followers' shoes and ask yourself, "What do I like in the tweets of those I follow? What don't I like?" Most likely, you are drawn to tweets that catch your attention, are clearly stated, and compel you to want more. After all, the best tweets are those that engage others, so be sure to infuse an element of engagement into your updates, too.

■ ■ ■ Skillful Merging of Business and Personal

Back to the matter of social media, I cannot overstate how important it is that you refrain from using Twitter to put forth a relentless stream of "buy my product" blasts into cyberspace. Certainly, the Twitter community is well aware of the business and networking potential of the tool. Twitter was, after all, created by Jack Dorsey to respond to a pressing business need shared by taxicab companies around the globe. However, those who use Twitter for more social purposes also want to be able to make use of the tool without a lot of high-pressure sales tactics coming at them from all directions. Think of how uncomfortable you become when you walk into a store and a salesperson immediately begins to follow you around, incessantly prattling on about this great product and that great deal and the limited-time offer you simply must take advantage of today. Odds are that within five minutes of browsing, you're ready to jump out of the store window just to escape the trap you've unwittingly wandered into. With Twitter, you want to similarly welcome folks to your tweet stream but then allow them to "browse a bit," as it were, giving them opportunity to ask for more information when *they're* ready for it.

Beyond assuring your Twitter followers that you're not an aggressive, ankle-biting salesperson, you also want to engage them in a way that welcomes them to find out more about you—not just about your product or service. After all, good business isn't about hard, emotionless sales pitches or shrill, in-your-face product announcements. It's about people engaging with other people to conduct transactions or other such exchanges. As such, when you're tweeting, present yourself as a real person with real interests. Let your followers know you have genuine curiosity about them and care for them. You needn't be patronizing or otherwise insincere; just be engaged. Here are a few things to think about as you look to get a little bit more "personal" when conducting business via Twitter:

- **Find common ground.** Whenever possible and practical, try to post updates that will be universally enjoyed and understood by your followers. Listen to your followers via their responses to determine what you have in common with them and touch on such matters on a regular—though not necessarily daily—basis.
- **Strive to make your business or brand more "human."** This is key to genuinely winning the hearts and minds of your followers,

who someday might become your customers or clients. Engage with them on a personal level, and even consider publishing a humanistic "mission statement" about your business somewhere on your blog or website (but don't attempt to tweet that!). As you tweet, keep your mission statement at the forefront of your mind and allow it to penetrate some of your updates.

- **Share personal information, but not private details.** Remember that Twitter is a public forum, so refrain from sharing private details about your life or the lives of others with your list of followers. If you feel the need to communicate on a deeper level with a follower, take that communication off the public page by using the direct message feature.

- **Do you need a disclaimer?** If you feel you need to take a stance on an issue that has proven controversial or polarizing, you might wish to add a disclaimer to your related tweets on the subject. Better yet, if you think your assertions could fan some flames of furor, ask yourself if it is really necessary to post them and risk alienating a sizable portion of your audience.

While the key to success on Twitter is reaching a wide audience to increase your business or brand visibility, remember that it's still a social setting. Respect the fact that some folks are on Twitter simply to connect and commune. If you skillfully blend a little of "you" into your business, you'll find you attract and retain a following that's truly interested in what you have to offer.

▪▪▪ Twitter Etiquette: Some Dos and Don'ts

You likely expected this topic to come up sooner or later. After all, this is *social* media we're discussing, and as with every social sphere, there is a code of conduct on Twitter that users should adhere to in order to be good members of the Twitterverse. You have already read about some of Twitter's rules, which constitute the actual terms of use you must agree to uphold, lest Twitter close your account for misuse (refer to that discussion in Chapter 2). What follows, however, is a list of the seven key articles of Twitter etiquette, which the Twitterverse has come forward to proclaim and communally support. At the same time that you're ensuring your tweets are on key, be sure you're singing in a tune that's generally acceptable to those around you.

- **Avoid becoming a mass follower.** Yes, this is how many of the "get thousands of Twitter followers in just one day" marketers appeal to newbies, but most genuine users know a scam when they see one. If your profile shows that you're following thousands of other Twitter users but have only a few followers of your own, you'll be blocked by others in a hurry. Choose whom you follow carefully and filter out whom you allow to follow you. In the end, your followers will be seen by those you follow and, if you're playing a strictly spammy numbers game, any real followers you might have hoped to attract will leave you in a heartbeat.
- **Tweet frequently but not incessantly.** If you tweet too often, your tweets will overrun the tweet feed of your followers, making it difficult for them and their other followers to follow a discussion. Don't tweet unless you have something truly useful or interesting to say, and keep the back-and-forth chirps (such as "oh, yeah," "me too," and "been there, done that") limited to direct messaging conversations that others don't need to wade through.
- **Avoid abbreviations whenever possible.** Although this was mentioned already, really take to heart that such cyber-speak is indicative of the younger set online and not what most would like— or expect—from a businessperson.
- **Avoid profanity in your tweets.** Given that language is full of so many words and concise phrases, colorful language isn't needed to establish your mood or sentiment. Save that that kind of edgy talk for direct interactions, not for the public forum.
- **Don't be a name-dropper.** Some folks get uncomfortable if they see their actual name referenced on Twitter. If you are replying

to a follower in the public tweet stream, keep the information suitable for all eyes and avoid sharing personal information about that follower.

- **Don't retweet your own posts excessively.** Unless there's something truly relevant that needs to be reposted, avoid reposting your own updates, lest your followers become bored and annoyed with seeing your tweet stream overrun by reruns.

- **If you need to focus on a topic (such as a special project, event, or so forth) that would be of interest to only *some* of your followers, establish another Twitter account simply to update about that topic.** In this way, those truly interested can follow your more specific updates on that account while the rest of your followers are not forced to read updates that are of little use to them.

The most important takeaway from this discussion of keeping your tweets on key is to ensure you're remaining true to your original tweeting purpose and are faithfully serving your audience of followers. By continually checking up on the construction and content of your tweets, you'll avoid the embarrassment of having your followers proclaim they no longer care about what you're doing.

8

Hashing Out Hashtags

So you know how to construct a compelling tweet, can excellently time and pace your tweets, and have an active following that can barely wait for your next message. In a word, you're a Twitter *success*. But with all the activity brewing on your Twitter home page, including all the tweets you have sent and the dialogue those updates have generated, how are you supposed to gain an end-to-end view of the discussion at hand? It's simple, really. With the press of just a single character on your keyboard, you can easily and effortlessly gather your topic-centric tweets in a way that helps you keep tabs on what you've posted. What's more, the inclusion of this character in your tweets will help your followers zero in on those topics you tweet about that are of interest to them. What character? It's the *hashtag*.

Is It All Just Hash?

Curiously, hashtags have proven to be more than just a bit mysterious to many in the Twitterverse, regardless of whether they are new or experienced Twitter users. Perhaps all the confusion is due to the offhand and casual manner they're spoken of by those in the know. Or maybe the mystery surrounding hashtags is thanks to the fact that this cryptic character sometimes appears in tweets without notice or even consistent structure. Whatever the reason may be, don't concern yourself if you aren't yet familiar with that term—hashtag—because you're certainly familiar with its character representation: "#." This is the "hash mark," but you might also know it as the "pound sign," the "number sign," or a "crosshatch." All you need to understand about this character as it appears in the Twitterverse is that it is the oft-mentioned hashtag, and you'll see it used as in this sample tweet: *So now even 6-year-olds seek worldwide fame and glory on the web. Well done, #balloonboy*.

Notice the hashtag in the preceding tweet: "#balloonboy." This is a tweet marker that makes it easy for folks to follow all the Twitter messages that are sent about the six-year-old boy from Colorado who was thought to be trapped in an oversized runaway balloon. All they need to do is search for "#balloonboy" from their Twitter search box to find, read, and respond to all related tweets that include that same hashtag. If any of them think that some of their followers might also be interested in any one or all of the tweets that are hashtagged "#balloonboy," they needn't retweet these messages. Instead, they can simply reference the hashtag in a tweet to their followers, as in this tweet: *I'm following the details of the boy apparently adrift in a balloon. Hashtag is #balloonboy*. So, to ensure you have a clear understanding of how the term is used within Twitter, a hashtag is a word or series of characters immediately preceded by the hash mark—as in *#balloonboy*.

Why use a hashtag? Plainly put, it's an organizer that folks in the Twitterverse implicitly agree to use and reference when tweeting about a particular topic. In this way, the members of the Twitter community converge to discuss a topic and then, in true communal fashion, adopt the hashtag to make it easy to follow and advance the discussion. With that said, you might wonder *when* a hashtag is truly useful. As in the case of the previously referenced October 2009 news story, wherein Twitter users employed the hashtag *#balloonboy* to track the frantic search for a six-year-old Colorado boy thought to have been carried off by a hot-air balloon, hashtags allow people to follow breaking news events of widespread interest and then offer information or assistance, if possible. So, when dire situations or oncoming threats arise, folks can insert hashtags into their related tweets to increase the search-ability of the information and breaking details they are sharing. The same holds true when popular-culture discussions related to bands, television shows, or movies pop up; Twitterers can insert hashtags that reference their favorite shows or bands into their tweets so that other fans can delve deep and follow along in their latest entertainment passions. The handy hashtag is good for business, too. Some companies will develop their own hashtags so that their followers can easily stay abreast of their business activities, promotions, and new product launches.

▪▪▪Using Hashtags

Now that you know what a hashtag is and a few of the ways it is put to work, here are a few things you should know about creating and using them for your own purposes.

- **Before creating your own hashtag, first search Twitter using the tweet search box on the main page to see if it already exists.** Try searching a few variations of the term you intend to use. If you find a close match that already relates to what you want to tweet about via the tag, you might want to simply adopt the existing tag and tweet your followers to inform them that you're tracking the topic. Otherwise, create you own tag and move ahead with your topic-specific stream.
- **Since the purpose is to include the hashtag in your tweets and encourage your followers to insert it into their related tweets, keep the hashtag as short but as intelligible as possible.** A good rule is to keep the hashtag to about 15 characters or fewer, which will allow you to use the remaining 125 characters of the tweet to include a helpful message.

- **If you want to create a hashtag to help your followers track you or your business at an event or conference, be sure to select and publish your hashtag well in advance so that your followers will know how to search for your related tweets.** As previously mentioned, retweet your hashtag notification message prior to the event, as well as a few times just as the event or conference is commencing, just to make sure your followers know how to find your related tweets.
- **Although you can't control how others include the hashtag in their responsive tweets, you should establish consistency in the method that *you* include it in your messages.** Some like to include the hashtag at the beginning of a tweet, while others prefer to position the tag at the end of the message. Whichever method you like best, use it and stick to it. Doing so makes for a cleaner hashtagged tweet stream. Avoid hashtagging in the middle of your tweet, since this method only disrupts the message you are trying to convey.

As you might expect, there are a few no-nos to avoid when using hashtags. Take care to keep from broaching these key points of hashtag protocol:

- **First and foremost, don't overuse the hashtag.** If you make a habit of including hashtags in all (or even in the greater majority) of your tweets, you lessen the true value of the tag, which is namely to help your followers sift out specific tweets about a certain topic.
- **Don't make your hashtag difficult to understand.** Ensure that you contextualize it in a way that makes sense to the specific topic you are tweeting about. If you intend to tweet about your activity at a trade show, create a tweet that includes your company name or purpose at the show (such as the preview of James Cameron's film *Avatar* at the San Diego Comic Convention: *#avatarpreview*).
- **Don't overlook the need to announce that you will be using a specific hashtag before you put it into use.** If you're going to

tweet about a new product's development and believe it will interest your followers, announce the new tag in your tweet stream and then repeat that announcement a couple of times so latecomers will understand your intent.

- **Don't begin using hashtags unless you're certain you will continue posting a useful and fluent stream of tweets that are specific—and interesting—to the topic you're tagging.** Put another way, don't implement a hashtag and then abandon it as quickly as you launched it.

- **Don't use the hash-mark symbol in one of the more conventional ways within your tweets.** That is, refrain from posting tweets like this: *Hey—our team is now #1 in the league*, or, *If you have questions, please call us directly at our phone # 123-4567.*

▪▪▪ Hashtag Helpers

If you're still a bit uncertain about hashtags or about how to find or follow them, you'll be happy to know that there are many hashtag helpers out there. The following are some of the better tools available to help you hash it all out.

▪▪ WHAT THE TREND? (HTTP://WHATTHETREND.COM)

Similar to opening the morning paper or turning on the daily news to see what's happening in current events, What the Trend? is a site that tracks the hot topics of the Twitterverse (see Figure 8-1). Visit the site to see what hashtagged keywords are trending in the highest volumes, and you will find that the majority of the hashtags listed are being used to reference timely or otherwise high-attention topics. Each topic has an active link embedded into the keyword or hashtag of interest that takes users directly to the Twitterverse so they can begin following along right away. Each topic also includes a summary that is actively edited and updated by the using community to help you understand why the topic is trending.

Figure 8-1. At What the Trend? you'll get an up-to-the-minute view of what's trending high in the Twitterverse, hashtags and all.

■ ■ HASHTAGS.ORG

While this isn't the most stylish of sites, Hashtags.org offers fast access to information about Twitter trends, top hashtags, and most-discussed people. Visit the site and either search for a term or click one of the right-hand navigation words to see what's abuzz in the global tweet stream. When you analyze the hashtag trends (as shown in Figure 8-2), you'll see the most-used tags, the tag itself (which is an active link to the tweet stream), and how many messages have referenced the topic in the past two months. The value here is that not only can you quickly find what's trending, but you can also determine the effectiveness of particular tags to determine how you might best develop some of your own.

Figure 8-2. Simple yet effective access to trends and hashtags; that's what Hashtags.org has in store for you.

▓ ▓ Tagalus (tagal.us)

If you're looking for more information about the meaning of any particular hashtag, since not all tweeters create immediately intelligible tagging terms, Tagalus is your dictionary of hashtags. Visit the site and submit a hashtag you've seen but don't quite understand, and Tagalus will help you find related tags and offer user-provided definitions of each (see Figure 8-3). If you have developed a new tag of your own that you hope will gain attention within the Twitter community, navigate over to the definition section on the Tagalus website to establish and explain your hashtag so that others can best understand its purpose.

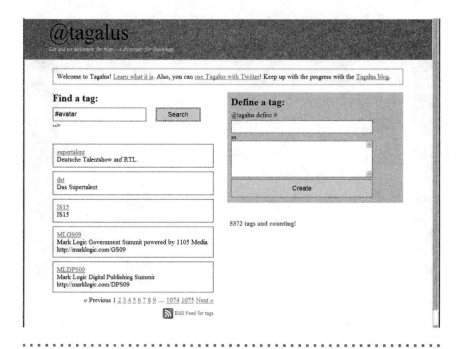

Figure 8-3. Tagalus is a hashtag dictionary that helps you understand what some of those cryptic tags really mean.

Of course, there are plenty more sites and tools devoted to hashtags—so many that you could easily become overwhelmed as to which one to use—but the few tools I just offered will help you establish familiarity and comfort with hashtags. As you begin to use them and possibly adopt a tool or two to better utilize them, you'll develop your own rhythm and reason for how and when you'll launch a hashtag.

9

Networking with Twitter

Now that you have set up your Twitter account, established a schedule for your tweeting, learned how to attract and maintain a solid audience of followers, and are consistently posting engaging and informative tweets, you may find yourself asking, "Well, if that isn't networking, what is?" You're right; you've been laying the building blocks for solid networking within the Twitterverse and elsewhere. After all, whenever you make yourself and your business available and accessible to a large population and then actively engage members of that population—not only for the purposes of selling to them but also to query, learn from, and interact with them—you are networking. But while we could call this chapter a wrap right now and assert that we already are networking just by claiming membership to the Twitter community, there are still some nuances to networking—especially via Twitter—that you'll want to understand in order to continue improving the method of your business-based tweeting. No matter the nature of your business—be it high tech or low key—you probably already know how important it is to make new contacts, sustain existing relationships, and work collaboratively with others to get the most out of others and give the most of yourself, your products, and your services. But do you know how to apply these basic networking principles to Twitter? Let's look closer at the finer points of networking within Twitter and find out.

■■■ Just Friends?

The advent of social media technology—that is, websites like Classmates.com, MySpace, Facebook, and so on—has brought a renewed interest in connecting people with people. Originally conceived as a way to "catch up" with long lost friends and acquaintances, the mindset quickly morphed into a way for younger folks to easily chatter with one another about just about everything (and often about nothing at all). Regardless of how they are used, social media portals like those just mentioned have made it remarkably easy for people to join together. While it makes sense to enjoy these tools as a source of "social downtime," the business relevance of such easy outreach and connection cannot be overstated. Because so much of the yakking that goes on within social networks is "have you heard about this" or "have you tried that," there's good reason to engage in that friendly conversation, hopefully motivating others to talk about the product or service *you're* offering.

For this reason, among others, "friending" in the social media universe entails so much more than simply passing the time in idle chitchat. Some have asserted the social media phenomenon is only an enormous time sink; when you "friend" somebody, you are tasked with attending to that person from that day forward. If you aren't actively engaging such friends in some manner, they will likely become bored or offended (or perhaps both) and will "defriend" or "unfollow" you. And if you say "good riddance" to them, you've just engaged in bad business. Business *is* an exercise in sociable behavior, in being friendly and useful to others. If you're not, why would patrons take a peek into your store or site? Why would they consider ever returning? And why would they bother to tell others about you? Social media is all about access, and the more access you give the public, the more interest you'll generate in others. Therefore, when you're being friendly enough to answer the question "what's happening?" on a regular basis, you're offering them access into what it is you do, what it is you sell, and why your business is something curious passersby would want to become a part of.

Consider the brick-and-mortar shopkeeper, the one who posts signs or announcements on his shop window, hoping to catch the attention of people on the street. If they're intrigued enough to venture over for a closer look, they'll probably peek into the window just to see what's inside. Similarly, you will gain the attention of others by posting short blurbs about your business on the Internet. Now, if your shop door is locked shut, curious onlookers won't be able to come inside for an even closer look. They'll quickly become disinterested or frustrated, and then they'll move on. Of course, if your door is open (as it should be), you can properly greet them and engage them in additional conversation, maybe about the weather, the big game tonight, that great movie playing at the theater around the corner, and, oh, maybe you can talk to them about your products, too. With Twitter, you're able to post those inviting messages on the virtual storefront window, attract others' attention, and then engage them in further friendly talk once they've ventured into your establishment. If they've enjoyed their time with you, they'll probably come back—and they might bring a friend or two as well. Summed up, social engagement is not a waste of time at all, but rather a core necessity in establishing and maintaining a customer base.

The very important flip side of "access" is that when you've properly engaged a visitor and let her know what you and your products are about, you also gain access to *her*. That is, when you establish a connection with a potential customer, she will be sure to tell you more about herself, what she does, and what she likes. Now you're discovering your customer's mindset and will be able to determine if your offerings are suitable to her and other customers' needs. Beyond this, you're also sure to engage customers who are businesspeople themselves, who might become future collaborators with you to the benefit of your business (and maybe to theirs, too). At last, you find the portal to networking through these so-called silly social media sites!

Now, to wrap up our discussion about access, take a moment to consider just how easy it has become to engage customers and collaborators via Twitter, thanks largely to how accessible the tool is to the greater public. As you've already learned from the preceding chapters, getting started and active on Twitter is incredibly easy and practically immediate. Since the learning curve is so shallow—that is, there isn't much setup or configuration required to get right to tweeting—folks can become active tweeters within minutes of signing up. Yes, you will need to weed out some of the Twitter activity that comes your way, as was discussed in Chapter 6, but even so, you will have access to a sizable audience like never before and will be able to engage that audience as a whole, through product or service announcements, or separately and discreetly for one-on-one business collaborations.

■■■ Is Mutual a Must?

Going back to the matter of managing your followers, the question that typically arises is whether it's important—or even necessary—to become a mutual follower of those who follow you. Without a doubt, the essence of being "social" involves reciprocity: I'll smile at you, but will you smile at me? Put more bluntly, some people look at being sociable to the extent of "what's in it for me." Indeed, we always want to receive a return on our investment, be it personal or professional in nature. In the realm of sales, for example, salespeople are constantly hunting for a good lead or potential deal and will pour effort out quickly to achieve a sale. If the lead or customer seems noncommittal or otherwise unwilling to reciprocate, the salesperson will redirect his attention to another possible customer. Although it sounds rather callous, businesses stay afloat not by wasting time on those who really haven't the intention or capability to close a deal, and the same holds true when it comes to networking using social media. With Twitter, then, a business should seek followers that will provide value—by way of revenue, interest, or access—to its bottom line. That said, is it necessary that a business become a follower to those who follow it? Sometimes yes, sometimes no. Yes, you should become a follower of those who follow you in these situations:

- They are actively engaging in your tweets in a way that's positive, productive, and even thoughtful.
- They have information that is useful to you that they've generously shared with you at your request.
- They post updates on their Twitter page that are of interest to you.
- They have been useful in retweeting some of your updates from their Twitter account.
- They have been instrumental in spreading the word about you to their friends.
- They're simply fun to follow.

As you can see, reciprocity isn't entirely based upon how much money a specific follower might contribute to your bottom line; judging your followers as such would be wrong and antithetical to the spirit of Twitter. Rather, if you find that you would characterize one of your followers by any of the foregoing attributes, especially to the point that they've successfully and genuinely engaged you, then clearly you should become one of their followers. That's what a healthy society is all about, right?

Conversely, there are those other times when it's not necessary that you become a follower of those who follow you. For example:

- Their updates are of no particular interest to you, and you're not certain why they chose to follow you. This could even be a follower to block later; wait and see.
- They haven't posted any responses to your updates.
- They haven't established a good rhythm for posting updates to their account.

- They have a tremendous number of followers already, and you feel as though you simply would be lost in the crowd.
- Their updates seem automated and disconnected from the responses they're receiving from their other followers.

These are just a few ideas of why or why not to follow someone that follows you. Like any social setting, your tastes and even friendships can and will change over time. Some followers will leave you, new followers will find you, and yet, through it all, you will certainly discover how to follow others in a way that builds a lasting engagement. The mutual follow isn't necessary, but it's a good thing to nurture when you find the right match.

■ ■ ■ Nurturing Your Network

While the concept of networking is by no means new, the method of staying connected with others via Twitter certainly is, so here are some Twitter-specific guidelines for maintaining your audience of followers. Like any friendship or business-customer relationship, continued positive interaction is dependent upon how well you engage and nurture those with whom you interact. Read through the following list of to-dos and ask yourself how effectively you have carried out these elements of your Twitter presence thus far.

- **Complete your account setup.** Post an image, set a theme, write a short bio, and show others what you and your business are all about. If you run with the default account settings for longer than a day (no kidding), you'll appear to the Twitterverse to be a rank newbie—or possibly a bot (a computer-based function that behaves on behalf of a human being to perform mundane tasks at top speed, usually for spammy purposes).
- **Post updates—now!** Get into the habit of posting updates—not all of them business- or product-related—to show some activity. You might not be attracting many followers at the beginning,

but why would you if you've just arrived and haven't explained who you are, what you do, and what you have to offer?

- **Maintain humbleness in your style.** If you think you'll attract attention by proclaiming yourself an Internet expert or social media know-it-all, you'll be alone to bask in your own greatness. Instead, note and share your interests but leave the back-patting to your followers; they'll tell you how great you are.

- **Maintain appropriate variety in your updates.** Don't push a product or service with every update. Recall the analogy of the shopkeeper with the few messages on the store window. To engage the customer who wanders in, you'll need to talk about *them* as much as (or possibly more) than you talk about *you*.

- **Keep your updates positive and open.** Avoid polarizing proclamations as much as possible and definitely refrain from arguing with your followers, especially within your tweet stream. Discussion is good, but keep it civil at all times. And remember, sometimes the best opinion is the one you keep to yourself.

- **On the heels of the previous point, be sure to be as engaging as possible.** While you needn't reply to every response you receive to your updates, you should enter into discussion with your followers on a regular basis. If not, you might unintentionally appear aloof.

- **Establish your persona (business or personal) and be consistent in that style.** If you vacillate between super chummy and uber-businesslike, you'll seem disjointed and disconnected. Be yourself—whoever you decide that should be—and maintain that style, especially if it has garnered you a good audience of followers.

As you grow more advanced in your Twitter use, you'll develop a rhythm that will guide your interactions with your followers and those whom you choose to follow. Don't think you need to be a Twitter power-networker right away; some of the best networking occurs organically. Be active, engaging, and mutual in your tweeting, and you'll soon find yourself in the company of a fun and fruitful network of other Twitterers.

10

Keeping Tabs on the Twitterverse

WITH SO MUCH ACTIVITY coursing through Twitter during every minute of every day, it might seem impossible to keep a pulse on what's happening at the site and how it involves or affects you, your business, or your brand. The fact is that it *is* impossible to monitor all the action on Twitter with an old-fashioned method of looking, searching, reading, and so forth. But that doesn't mean you can simply ignore what other people are talking about on Twitter, as doing so is a surefire recipe for lessening the effectiveness of your Twitter use. The good news, though, is there are plenty of third-party tools to help you keep an eye on of what's being tweeted and stay informed when the tweets are for or about you and your business. In this chapter, you'll get a tour of some of the best tools that help others just like you keep tabs on the Twitterverse by monitoring Twitter.

■■■ Why Keep Tabs Anyway?

Before we jump into a discussion of some of the most useful and "socially" accepted tools that help users keep a pulse on Twitter activity, we first need to understand *why* it's important to monitor tweet traffic. If you actively manage brands, imprints, or products, you already know that when you keep an eye and an ear open to what folks are saying about your offerings, you're able to provide close to immediate input and assistance. You can even perform potential damage control when others are talking about you or your brand, company, or product.

As an example, consider the matter of a blogger who is trying to imbed a new tool or widget into his blog, but trouble abounds when he discovers a puzzling compatibility problem. Since he's also tweeting actively to let his readers know what he is doing, he mentions the snag he's run into and also mentions the widget by name. Elsewhere, the developer of the widget is actively scanning tweets for mention of his product, and this blogger's tweet pops up. Immediately, the widget provider responds to the blogger's tweet and offers guidance and a resolution to the compatibility problem. The blogger successfully completes the integration and then goes on to tweet to his followers about the good experience he has had with the widget provider and the value of the nifty widget he has now embedded into his blog. The widget provider has not only been able to monitor potential integration problems with his tool, but he can now use the experience to improve the integration instructions that are included with his widget. What's more, he's also reached out to help a user of the widget with active and attentive customer service while enabling the blogger to publicly sing the praises of the widget, its features, and the caring company behind it. Had the widget provider not made himself aware of the troubled tweet, the discussion could have gone forward in a way that would paint the widget as difficult, cumbersome, and probably not the best widget available (for example, "Same problem here. I switched to WidgetX because it was easier.").

■■■ Tools to Keep Track

You get the idea. Keeping tabs on the Twitterverse in this way helps you sustain your brand or product, improve its usefulness and functionality, and become visible in your support of it. In this way, you can actively perform damage control on conversations or complaints so that they do not spread significantly or reach you only after a negative sentiment has begun to take root. Instead, you're on the front lines and can quell any troubles or misconceptions at the moment they are uttered. *That's* why it's important to keep tabs on the Twitterverse. Read on, now, for some of the best third-party tools (that is, developed outside of Twitter itself) that help you do just this.

■ ■ TWEET SCAN (HTTP://TWEETSCAN.COM)

Tweet Scan is a live search engine for sifting through Twitter activity (see Figure 10-1). If you want to search for a topic or name and see what's being said about it, Tweet Scan allows you to enter your search term of interest, and it does the rest. When it finds tweets containing your search term, it will display them for you. And if you're too busy to sit by your computer and manually search and review matches, Tweet Scan allows you to register for e-mail notification every time your term is mentioned. You can even stream the activity surrounding your search term to your computer via an RSS feed. Those who have used this tool proclaim it to be a great time-saver and an excellent way to keep pulse of what others might be saying about your business or brand (as previously explained). It's not flashy to behold, yet its beauty is in its results.

Figure 10-1. Tweet Scan is a favored third-party tool for monitoring tweets containing specific topics.

■ ■ TWEETBEEP (HTTP://TWEETBEEP.COM)

TweetBeep is another highly regarded tweet-monitoring tool for tracking mentions of your business or brand, but it is most effective for finding business leads and collaborators (see Figure 10-2). So, say that you are a real estate agent and you decide to use TweetBeep to monitor for terms relevant to your business. TweetBeep will help you with tasks like indentifying and connecting with people who are looking to buy a home or even locating properties for sale in the locale that you service. With TweetBeep, you can elect to receive daily or hourly e-mail updates of matches to your searches.

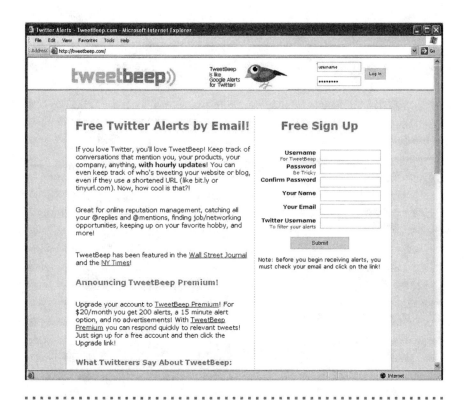

Figure 10-2. TweetBeep is yet another tool for tracking tweets that are related to your business or the sort of service or product you offer.

▪▪ FRIENDFEED (HTTP://FRIENDFEED.COM)

If ever you wanted to be able to track activity of your friends, customers, or collaborators when they're not directly interacting with you (or even talking about you on Twitter), FriendFeed provides you access to this information (see Figure 10-3). With FriendFeed, you can track where your best customers, associates, and trusted friends are traversing online and discover what they discover by viewing their postings on Twitter, Flickr, blogs, and so on. Even if they're not telling you directly, you can still keep pulse on what else they are doing and saying through FriendFeed.

Figure 10-3. FriendFeed lets you track the postings and tweets of your trusted friends and associates so you can discover what they discover.

TWEETBURNER (HTTP://TWEETBURNER.COM)

You've been actively tweeting and posting tweet-friendly shortened Web links in the hopes that your followers will follow them to your business's home page, but how will you know if those links are being used? With Tweetburner, you get a highly useful three-in-one tool that provides analytical data regarding the URLs you embed in your tweets (see Figure 10-4). Not only is it a URL-shortening tool (like TinyURL or bit.ly), but it also allows you to track the click rate of the shortened

Figure 10-4. Tweetburner shortens long URLs and then provides click-rate analytics.

URLs you've tweeted. Finally, it lets you track the most active shortened URLs that are serviced by Tweetburner, giving you insight into the popularity of links others have created and tweeted.

■ ■ TINKER (HTTP://TINKER.COM)

Tinker is a newer tool that allows you to monitor "event streams" of conversations on Twitter, FriendFeed, and Facebook (see Figure 10-5). With Tinker, you can track the activity of any event, announcement, or breaking news item that is abuzz across social media networks. By following Tinker's trends, you can see how some events or announcements gained and spurred activity, as well as those that maybe never received their hoped-for attention.

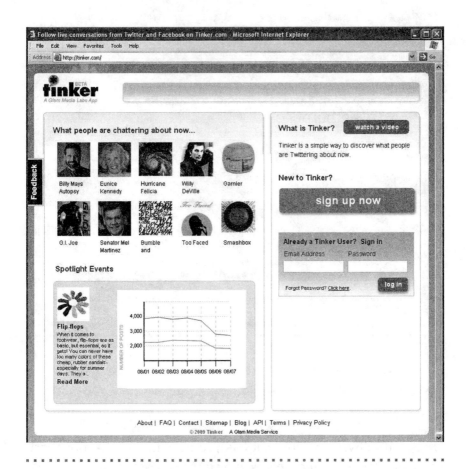

Figure 10-5. Tinker allows you to follow "event streams" to track consumer and social networking trends and reactions to events and news activity.

■ ■ ExecTweets (http://exectweets.com)

Are you the sort of person who is curious to see what big-business executives are tweeting about? Do you look to learn from the success stories of those who have climbed the business ladder? Then take a look at ExecTweets. Notable company executives from the likes of Best Buy, Microsoft, Zappos.com, and more are actively tweeting, provid-

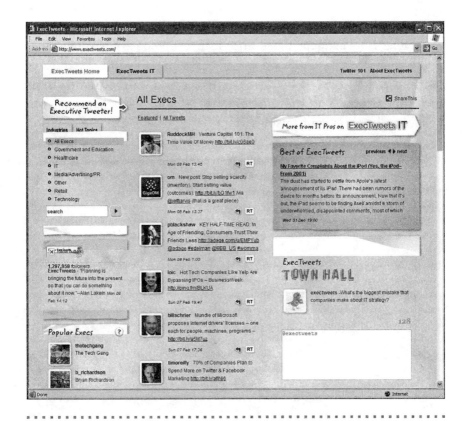

Figure 10-6. See what the movers and shakers are saying by checking in on them with ExecTweets.

ing their thoughts and observations on the business realm (see Figure 10-6). Why not listen in to find out if you see and think like they do? This is an especially useful way to see how the most successful businesspeople engage with their customers, as well as how the topics they tweet about make or shape their businesses.

If the preceding review of useful third-party Twitter tools and sites seems a bit overwhelming, consider that there are so many more out there for you to explore. You needn't cultivate an expertise in each and every one, but you should be aware of the sorts of services that each offers. Investigate these and scan cyberspace for others that pique your interest. Settle on what seems to suit you best and use that tool for a while, at the same time keeping an eye on new sites and improvements in the existing sites. If you find a tool that you believe will propel your business in a better way, make use of it and maybe even tweet your followers about what you've discovered.

11

Twenty-Five Business Uses for Twitter

As we wrap up this section of the book, it's time for a rapid-fire overview of some of the best business uses for Twitter. You've learned how to access Twitter, create an account, craft compelling tweets, and keep a pulse on the Twitterverse. In this regard, you know *how* to Twitter, but you might still be wondering about *where, when,* and *why* to Twitter—at least I hope you are, since it's imperative that you constantly tend to your intended purpose for and expected outcome from tweeting. You also might still be wondering if harnessing Twitter really will be beneficial to your business. To that end, get ready to put your wondering aside, as what follows is a list of the top twenty-five business uses for Twitter. Read through each idea and suggestion, and you just may find or refine your niche within the Twitterverse while learning new ways to maximize the accessibility and exposure of your brand or business.

■■■1. Brand Proliferation

As you have already learned, one of the most compelling reasons businesses decide to harness the power of Twitter is to improve their brand awareness, exposure, and management. Indeed, companies need only a well-thought-out tweeting plan before they can actively and immediately begin establishing, refining, and sometimes even revitalizing their brands on Twitter. So, if you or your company needs to get a firmer grip on your brand proliferation, become an active and present tweeter on a regular and reliable basis while avoiding tweeting your brand messaging too aggressively.

In doing so, not only will your brand awareness grow organically through the flow of your well-crafted and well-timed messages, but you also will be able to stay up-to-date on what the Twitterverse is saying about you and your brand. After you see how you're being perceived, you can then analyze what steps you can take to bolster or even correct the course of conversation that shapes the public's perception of what you and your brand represent.

■■■2. Real-Time Feedback

Naturally, when you launch a new product, unveil a cutting-edge feature, or simply make an announcement, you are eager to know how your news has been received. It was not long ago that businesses had to wait weeks, even months to track consumer feedback, but with Twitter, you can tweet your news and gain feedback almost instantaneously. Even receiving no Twitter feedback over the course of a few days is "feedback" in its own way, in that it indicates that not one Twitterer noticed or cared enough about your news to respond. Utilize the immediacy of Twitter to determine what works and what doesn't for your business by tracking the Twitterverse's response (or lack thereof) to your tweeted announcements. When you do receive feedback, it isn't necessary that you respond to each and every message. You can, however, monitor how Twitterers react to your news and determine if there's a trend forming that you can address collectively.

With Twitter, businesspeople have access to a feedback mechanism that has eluded them until now: the ability to directly engage with their customers one-on-one. Feedback is your daily, weekly, monthly, and annual report card; regard it highly and learn from it daily.

■ ■ ■ 3. Talent Scouting and Acquisition

The advent of the Internet has made it easier to locate and get in contact with service providers that offer specific skills or talents, but it also has made the search process far more transparent. Indeed, whereas businesses once could only judge a service provider by its résumé, now they can take the public's pulse on who's who in a particular field of service and instantly access recommendations and reviews of providers in their area. With Twitter, businesses have learned to post an inquiry for assistance or referral, sometimes making direct contact with a prospective service provider (great!) and sometimes seeking input from others regarding which provider can best solve their particular problem (better yet!). If you're in need of graphic design, Web authoring, clever copywriting, or maybe just a good electrician in your local area, tweet your request and watch how the Twitterverse comes out to answer your call.

■ ■ ■ 4. Industry News and Trends

It's certainly liberating that the Internet has given us access to such a wealth of information, whether from news sites we navigate to or social networks we are members of. However, it's downright enabling that Twitter has given us access to what *other people* have found as they have dug around online for information that is of interest to them. Indeed, as you have seen, many Twitterers actively embed links to articles and other postings of interest that you can follow to see what's buzzing and why. With this access, you can learn what's happening in your area of business specialty, what trends are emerging, and what attitudes about them might be shifting. You'll also discover where there are product or service gaps, which stand as opportunities for you to step forward and fulfill as-yet unserviced needs. In this sense, Twitter is a hotbed of both mainstream and alternative information, wherein you can peer into your particular industry from every possible perspective. And when you harness the conversation streams that run through Twitter, you get up-to-the-minute details about where you and your business can focus and succeed.

■ ■ ■ 5. Collaboration

At nearly no other point in time do communication tools like Twitter better show their true worth than when they're used to facilitate business collaborations. Indeed, Twitter easily enables businesspeople to engage in virtual "collective thinking" to brainstorm business ideas, solve pressing problems, or seize forthcoming opportunities. No matter whether a small group of colleagues wants to conduct a private business conversation via tweets or a business wishes to reach out to the larger public to actively solicit ideas and input, Twitter's short-burst, back-and-forth, collaborative environment allows users to quickly and efficiently address issues and assess opportunities. Furthermore, when the public is allowed to chime in, collaborative tweeting enables businesses to engage their customer base and garner their help and support on new initiatives.

■ ■ ■ 6. Customer Service

Picture this undesirable situation: A very vocal customer is standing at the customer-service window in a store, banging away at the tinny silver bell, yet he is unable to draw the attention of anyone at the obviously abandoned counter. The customer then raises his voice and begins to grouse about the "lousy service and terrible products" at the store. Eventually he begins attracting the attention of the other customers browsing through the store, some of whom disregard the spectacle while others listen and maybe even begin to ally with this disgruntled patron. Soon a small group of individuals takes up the crusade to find someone—anyone—to hear their grievances. Many other customers have already left the store, sure never to return in the future for fear of being confronted by another similarly uncomfortable situation. Of course, there's nothing extreme about this situation; it happens all too often. With Twitter, however, the attentive businessperson can monitor for this sort of customer dissatisfaction and can step in quickly to rectify the problem, likely turning the unhappy patron into a lifelong follower because the response to the matter was swift and personal. Better yet, a business can use Twitter to proactively post useful information and updates to customers, which will help them identify and resolve problems that have yet to rear their ugly heads.

■■■ 7. Lead Generation

Simply stated, a "lead" is another term for a potential customer that might be interested in your products or services, and with Twitter, you can actively seek out and court leads in a way that encourages them to make a transaction. All you need to do to sell products to those who are not yet convinced they need them is first work to understand their need or desire and then present yourself as a respected and trustworthy provider.

When you scan the Twitterverse for tweets that contain keywords relevant to your brand or business, you find people who are talking freely about what you offer. Some Twitterers will even actively indicate their desire to purchase a particular product or service—if only they could find someone to serve them. It is likely that these Twitterers have said aloud what it is that they are looking for in the hopes that someone within earshot would step forward to say, "I can help you with that," so this is your chance to offer your assistance. Approach hot leads like these carefully and engage them calmly, and you might just end up with a sale.

■■■ 8. Lost and Found

Here's a unique use of Twitter that is simply too clever to leave unmentioned: When you picture a traditional "lost and found," you rightly imagine a large cardboard box full of all manner of items that folks have left behind in a store, at an event, and so forth. It's up to the person who has lost one of her belongings to retrace her steps and ask if the item has been recovered. When it comes to Twitter— and especially the real-time Twittering that participants at conferences and conventions engage in—it is not uncommon to see tweets like "Just found a BlackBerry at our booth—if you lost yours, please return to identify." How helpful is that? Sure, a single altruistic tweet won't grow your brand or business tenfold, but it's one of the most socially genuine ways to use the tool.

■■■ 9. Directing Traffic

Twitter can be an incredibly effective tool for launching word-of-mouth campaigns that will help more people find your business—especially if you are offering a special deal or promotion to your followers or have a unique event underway. Tweet the breaking news associated with your brand or product and watch your active followers retweet that message to their friends. Carefully message your followers to "tell friends who might not have received this news," and watch how quickly the news travels.

■ ■ ■ 10. Limited-Time Offers

Following the points made under item 9, you can use Twitter to indicate limited-time offers, post online coupon codes, and broadcast special promotions to maximize sales of products that have a time-sensitive appeal or usefulness. Tweet that today's special won't be available tomorrow, so hurry over before it's gone. Regardless of what you're selling, limited-time offers motivate customers to purchase almost any product or service, and Twitter is a great tool for getting the word out fast and gaining fast response.

■ ■ ■ 11. Event Updates and Pre-Alerts

As mentioned in the item 8, Twitter is very effective when it is used to cover the minute-by-minute details of conferences, conventions, and other such events. Businesses in attendance tweet their whereabouts and what they're doing so attendees can follow along. Many businesses will tweet an update like, "I'm in exhibit bldg C—first to find me gets a free widget." Believe it or not, this sort of fun engagement works.

■ ■ ■ 12. Meeting Organization

Twitter is a great tool for company and project teams who want to meet up on the fly, because it enables users to send direct messages to one another, such as, "Hey, quick meeting at Coffee Beanz in 10 min." Other team members can acknowledge that they're on their way, while those individuals who cannot attend the meeting can stay abreast of the conversation virtually via real-time tweets that describe the topic under discussion.

■■■13. Note to Self

If you have ever written down an important piece of information only to find out that it went through the laundry the next day, consider sending a direct message to yourself. Many businesspeople use Twitter to send reminders to themselves, such as the details of important contacts they have just encountered. Others even send messages to themselves as they think of them, virtually building tomorrow's to-do list.

■■■14. Consultation

You've already read how Twitter allows you to provide immediate information and assistance to your customers, thereby enabling you to defuse potentially explosive customer-service situations. But have you considered that you can also use Twitter to dispense useful advice and guidance to your followers? If you're in a profession where your consultation *is* your product, you can augment your interactions and relationships with your clients by tweeting them—either publicly or via direct messages—the helpful and even critical information that they need.

■■■15. Test Marketing

Thanks to the Internet, businesses big and small have the ability to reach millions of potential customers worldwide and send out "test balloons" to determine if there's truly a market for products and services that are still in the development phase of production. As it happens, Twitter is the newest way to message this audience, and savvy businesses are polling their followers to find out if their ideas for new products and services have "legs." If your followers respond favorably, then the test succeeded. Furthermore, if the product or service that has garnered excitement from your followers is still under development, you can tweet them the daily details of the development process and keep them apprised of the forthcoming official launch.

■ ■ ■ 16. Rumor Control

Just as Twitter can be harnessed to improve a business's customer service efforts, it can also be used to provide frontline facts when rumors begin to swirl. Sometimes a rumor can be good for a brand or business, especially if it gathers excitement among potential customers, as in the case of the launch of a breakthrough product. Other rumors, however, can have near-immediate damaging effects. Either way, an attentive business can watch for rumors that are swelling in the Twitterverse and quickly chime in to steer the conversation in the appropriate direction. You can even get creative and start your own rumors about your business. Just be careful when doing so.

■ ■ ■ 17. Casual Interaction

True to the foundation upon which social media rests, Twitter allows businesses' brand or company spokespersons (or, better yet, owners) to engage in "water cooler" chitchat with their followers and customers on occasion. Do you recall our discussion of how to blend business and personal tweets from Chapter 7? If not, turn back to that chapter for advice on how to begin utilizing Twitter to casually interact with your customers. Doing so gives your customers the opportunity to ask questions within a safe setting and allows you to address any wants, needs, or concerns they may have that are related to your company or products. When you offer your customers this type of comfortable access, you'll find that your audience will become more deeply engaged with your company, brand, and products.

■■■ 18. Identity Development

When you interact with your customers by sending them business-related or more casual tweets, you help solidify their perception of your company or brand identity. Because Twitter encourages users to post stream-of-consciousness updates (some call it "life-streaming"), opportunities abound for you to post occasional mundane thoughts that will help round out your persona in the public's eye. Avoid establishing an identity that runs counter to your brand or business or becoming the tiresome perpetual pitchman. Instead, tweet updates that fully illuminate who you are and what you stand for in your business and personal life. Refrain from tweeting about polarizing matters whenever possible, but don't be afraid to let 'em know who you really are.

■■■ 19. Fact-Checking

By now you are aware that the tweet stream can provide you with near-immediate access to information, so use this knowledge to your advantage when you need some fast facts that matter to you and your business. Whether you're tracking an industry development, monitoring a perceived change in consumer attitude, or trying to authoritatively confirm a competitor's big announcement, when you tweet in search of facts, you will likely find an audience of followers who are ready to rally their friends to help you find the facts you are looking for.

■■■ 20. Listen to—and Learn from—Your Customers

Sometimes the best way a business can communicate is by passively *listening*, which is why it has been suggested that you not tweet incessantly but rather pace your tweets so you can gain response from your followers. When you drown your followers out with a barrage of your own tweets, you are indicating to them that you're not listening and that you're not very interested in what they—your followers, your customers—have to say. When you listen to them, you'll learn whether they're satisfied or not, and you'll also discover how well you're reaching them on their terms, in the way that they want to be engaged.

■■■ 21. Launch Opinion Polls or Informal Surveys

In order to hear from your customers, you might need to ask them an open-ended question first. Thankfully, Twitter is great for tweeting a question of the day, which will help you collect information about what your customers think of your products, company developments, and related news. You can also learn a lot about your followers from their level of response to the surveys themselves. Do you have thousands of followers but few reliable respondents? If so, it might be time to clean out those faux followers. Polls and surveys help you easily gather data about customer likes, dislikes, and methods of engagement.

■■■ 22. Product Safety and Customer Security

This one's quite important: If you have a product or service in which a safety matter has arisen or a customer security breach (in the case of an app or a widget) has been detected, use Twitter to help spread the word and provide cautionary or corrective guidance to your customers. Naturally, you would also communicate this information on your company website, blog, and wherever else you engage your clientele. Twitter, however, can certainly help you spread the word when time—and safety—are of the essence.

▪▪▪ 23. Internal Communications and Product Development

Some business teams have found Twitter's direct-message feature to be especially useful for providing real-time updates about a product under development. It also has been helpful in companies that utilize the product life-cycle method, wherein one team will add an element of value to the product before handing it off to another team for the next step of development. Tweeting these handoff points allows businesses to inform and motivate an entire group of employees with just a single message. In this way, valuable time is maximized every step of the way.

▪▪▪ 24. Augment Other Online Presences

While today there seems to be available a near plethora of communication and information-sharing tools and methods, the fact is that not everyone uses the same tool. Because of this, savvy businesses have embraced many social media platforms to reach the largest audience possible. With the advent of Twitter, businesses can communicate to those folks who would rather not sit by a computer monitor or who are on the go but would still like to receive breaking news as it occurs. By incorporating Twitter into a business's technology and outreach strategy, it's possible to reach more folks by way of the techno-tool they most prefer.

■ ■ ■ 25. Enjoy the Interaction

In this final point, it's useful—nay, imperative—that businesses and businesspeople today show passion and pleasure in their work. Consumers have become rightly choosy in how they'll spend not only their money but their time, too. If you're engaging in your Twitter approach and are relaxed enough to embrace the benefits of social interaction, your enjoyment will shine through in your messaging and further boost your business, its reputation, and your all-important bottom line.

PART 3

Advancing the Twitter Touch

12

Applying Elements of Viral Marketing

UNLIKE *FIELD OF DREAMS,* the sports film in which Kevin Costner's character is goaded into erecting a ballpark by the spirits of baseball past, who continually repeat the phrase "If you build it, they will come," real-world marketing isn't so straightforward. In fact, many businesses build online presences these days through websites, company blogs, marketing messaging, and so forth, and *still* nobody comes. So, what's a company to do? In order to successfully attract potential customers to your brand or business in this age of hyper-connectivity, you need to engage in *viral marketing,* an outreach approach in which you put the word out about a product, event, or service and then encourage the recipients of your message to tell their networks of friends—people you don't yet know yourself—about the news, too.

When your products and announcements are so compelling that not only do the initial message recipients fawn over them but they can't wait to tell their friends about them too, you've struck gold within the marketing realm. But just like mining for gold, you won't necessarily dig up a fortune with the first turn of the shovel. Don't let this discourage you, however, because Twitter gives you such an extensive reach that you can turn the first shovel and then suddenly find yourself surrounded by followers and their friends, each holding their own shovel and ready to help you dig.

■■■ Revisiting Viral Marketing

If it's been a while since you've thought about viral marketing—or perhaps it's a new concept to you—take a moment to acquaint yourself with this method and means of customer outreach. Viral marketing is a new-age term for the old standard: *word-of-mouth*. It's what you've been reading about in this book all along, working to put the word out about your brand, product, or service in the hopes that others will help you spread the good news. At their base, marketing messages become "viral" in the same way that a cold or the flu spreads from person to person; the originator of the virus need not be acquainted or in contact with a recipient further down the line to spread the germ. Perhaps you recall a practically unforgettable television commercial from the 1970s for Fabergé Organics shampoo (with wheat-germ oil and honey), in which the as-yet-unknown Heather Locklear proclaimed that she liked the shampoo so much that she told two friends, "and they told two friends, and so on, and so on, and so on . . ."

A visual representation of the way that viral messages spread from one person to the next and the exponential growth that results is depicted in Figure 12-1. The topmost "1" in the illustration that follows represents your originating message (in this context, your tweet), and the subsequent layers demonstrate just how many people a viral message can spread to, assuming each message recipient passes the news along to two friends.

Interestingly, that vintage hair commercial had true "stickiness" because its "and so on, and so on" message stuck in the viewer/listener's head. The key to creating a sticky marketing message, of

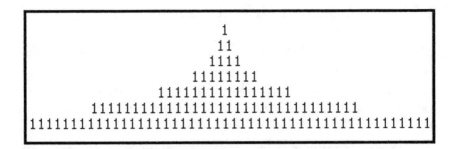

```
                      1
                     11
                   1111
                11111111
           1111111111111111
      11111111111111111111111111111111
1111111111111111111111111111111111111111111111111111
```

Figure 12-1. Viral marketing allows you to harness the power of the Twitterverse. Let your followers spread your message for you!

course, is to ensure that folks who repeat it truly remember the product it advertises. Because the shampoo advertised had a name that easily rolled off the tongue and included the intriguing ingredients of wheat-germ oil and honey, people remembered the product after the commercial had ended, and they would even cite the "and so on" phrase when they saw the product on a store shelf. Yes, I saw this happen on more than one occasion back in the day!

So, when you are developing a message about your brand or product, tweak and refine it until it is similarly compelling and repeatable, and you just might catch one of your customers reciting it when walking up to your product in a store. If this seems too simple to be true, remember that your message must be characterized by two important attributes: it must be contagious—irresistible and compelling—and it must reach those who have the greatest ability to pass it on to the most people, those known as influencers to a wide and diverse audience. This, of course, is the trick to successfully introducing a viral message to your followers and then on to the larger public. While there is no guarantee that every message you intend to be viral will actually catch hold, there are steps you can take to increase the likelihood that it does.

Developing a Viral-Friendly Message

While you have already learned how to craft a careful tweet, the following discussion will focus on how to construct a viral tweet that you hope your followers will retweet to their respective networks. And before you ask, no, not every one of your updates should be viral in nature. Your followers and customers will catch on quickly, and when they do, you stand to lose valuable relationships that you have been actively nurturing. But when you do want to attempt a viral tweet, consider the following tips and suggestions:

- **Make the message short, chirpy, and even rhythmic.** You don't need to make the message rhyme, but keep it interesting and easy to repeat. While your followers won't necessarily *say* it to others (they'll retweet it), they might repeat it over and over in their heads. Now is your opportunity to leverage and further establish your customers' perception of your company or brand identity, so tweet out these messages as organically as possible (wheat-germ oil and honey not necessarily required).
- **Ensure that the message is timely and fits in with your usual flow of tweeting.** That is, don't suddenly interrupt a discussion that's underway on your Twitter home page with a "commercial break."
- **Make sure your appeal is honest and reliable.** Avoid empty promises that you can't deliver. The bait-and-switch tactic is what has given used-car salesmen and Internet pitch jockeys the bad reputations they so richly deserve. If you're sending a viral message, make sure it is 100 percent accurate, lest the message that your recipients spread far and wide is that you or your brand are frauds. Avoid this like, well, the plague.
- **Include easy and immediate access to more information by embedding a compressed URL link into the message.** Let the tweet itself act as a teaser of sorts. It should be useful in its own right but should only be the tip of something even bigger and better that can be found at the embedded URL link.

Don't overthink or overdo your viral messages. Remember, you are still restricted to 140 characters in your tweets—and even less than that if you want to make it easy for your followers to pass the message along to two of their friends, and so on, and so on. . . .

■■■ Helping Your Followers Spread the Word

Following that last thought of making it easy for your messages to spread from person to person, you'll need to do most of the work for your followers and their friends if you hope to see your tweets go viral. Just as previous discussions have explored how to make retweeting a message simple by relieving retweeters of the burden of editing your original update, your viral tweet will also need to have some essential ingredients to help it along its viral way. Consider these pieces of advice:

- **Keep the message readable by folks of all social-media skill levels.** If you embed too many clever abbreviations, there is a chance that the message will only be readable by those who are steeped in the ways of SMS-speak. If you think you can be clever with abbreviations and still deliver a punchy and memorable message, think again. Your punch line will surely be lost on those who are not in-the-know—and you can't afford to lose that potential audience, ever.

- **Include the promise of a free product, an exclusive discount, or a limited-time offer within the message and be sure to fully deliver on that commitment when the message recipients come to collect on it.** Make sure to offer them a useful, compelling, or fun payoff for their attention and diligence, lest they groan about what a letdown your "special promotion" was and begin retweeting your viral update with a "don't waste your time" disclaimer.

- **Only extend honest messages to your followers.** After all, when followers forward your tweet along, they don't want their own credibility or good judgment to be called into question for having broadcast a red herring. If the message is real, relevant, and rewarding, it will be even easier for the recipients to forward it along to their networks.

If you deliver on a promise, maintain unwavering integrity in your appeal, and make it practically mindless for your followers to forward along a tweet, you'll improve the likelihood that the message will go viral. If your offer sounds too good to be true—yet it *is* true—your message is already well positioned to fan out not only across the Twitterverse but throughout greater cyberspace as well.

■■■ Putting Value on Referrals and the Referrers

Within the realm of social networking sites, the camaraderie of people sharing with people is the incentive for folks to engage in dialogue, step forward to help when a question arises, and make recommendations to those seeking the firsthand experiences and opinions of others. This spirit of communal sharing runs high when the conversation is chatty and, well, social. When it comes to market-based messaging, however, some folks will be tentative to engage when they're asked to pass the word along about a business, brand, or product.

Followers with whom you have previously developed and nurtured solid interpersonal relationships are generally inclined to respond to such messages along the lines of, "Sure, I trust you and I like you and your brand; I'll tell my friends." Sometimes, though, and especially when you get into the habit of too frequently asking these types of requests or favors—and that's what they are, as you are asking your followers to do you the favor of passing along a message you hope will go viral—your followers might begin to wonder, "What's in it for me?" And to be fair, why should they help you do your work without any sort of reward or compensation in return? Rather than risk wearing out your welcome or causing your followers to sigh aloud every time you come back to ask them for yet another favor, you'd be well advised to make their helpfulness worth their while. Why not show your followers how much you value referrals and extend rewards to the top referrers of your messages?

Referral rewards, as the marketing lingo coins it, are a tricky matter, especially within the social network stratosphere, where so many folks are wary of cheap marketers who are eager to exploit the otherwise open and sharing environment. However, if you have taken the time to establish and evolve your Twitter presence and have engaged your followers properly, they will be ready and eager to help spread your message when doing so gains them discounts, special offers, and targeted treatment. Easy enough, right? Just let them know you're happy to reward those who refer new customers or clients and then, when newcomers make a transaction, be sure to ask who referred them. Reward all referrers and let your newly referred customers know how you value this sort of assistance; they'll likely become your next referrers.

■ ■ ■ ■ ■ ■ ■ ■ ■ ■ ■ ■ ■ ■ ■ ■ ■

13

A Closer Look at the Need for Engagement

BY THIS POINT, YOU'VE learned that Twitter users generally occupy one of two extreme ends of the social networking continuum. On the one side are the "socialites," who feel that business-centric tweeters charge into the Twitterverse only to beat other users into consumer submission with their products, services, or ideas. On the other side are the "marketeers," who see Twitter as a time sink where lonely people converge to fill another twenty-four hours of their direction-less purpose by yakking all day about everything and nothing. To be sure, neither characterization is 100 percent accurate, but there's plenty to learn from these sharply opposing perceptions. As always, the truth of how any one social user or any one business tweeter intends to spend time each day on Twitter lies closer to the center of the social networking continuum, where users seek fulfilling interaction at the same time that they actively contribute valuable information or guidance to others. However, even those tweeters with the best of intentions can find themselves far off-course of where they had aimed to be.

Take a step back and analyze where your tweets currently fall within the social networking continuum. Are you socializing more than you are marketing, or vice versa? If your tweets are tending toward either extreme end of the social networking spectrum, whether you are socializing or marketing too much, the time has come for you to even out your tweeting strategy. When you strike a balance with your tweets, your proper and passionate engagement with others will also serve to generate revenue for your business, leaving both parties completely satisfied and pleased to come back for more. So, without further ado, let's get your tweets in harmony so that they can better sing to the needs, desires, and dreams of both you and your clients.

■■■ One More Look: Determining the Tweet That Is Best for Your Business—and Your Customers, Too

If you feel as though the discussions in this book often circle back to topics previously detailed in preceding chapters, you're right. I have been continually encouraging you to revisit your Twitter goals, intentions, and plan so that you don't temporarily lose sight of the grounding principles of your Twitter campaign in your excitement to try out the new tweeting techniques and strategies you read about in this book. And so, here again we return for a deliberate and detailed refresher on our original discussion points to ensure that you are comfortable and familiar with the concept of marketing within a real-time social networking setting. Consider these grounding points once again:

- **Again, establish whether Twitter is the right marketplace for you, your brand, and your business.** By this point in your reading, you have come to understand the Twitter community, discovered how its members communicate, and learned how they like to be engaged—and engage with others in return. Through this, perhaps you've learned that Twitter is the perfect setting for marketing what your business has to offer. It might even be a place where you, yourself, are flourishing, thanks to the very friendly and personable person-to-person and business-to-consumer Twitter interactions you have had. On the other hand, if you've reached this point in the book and for whatever reason have decided that Twitter is not an avenue you want to travel, that's fine, too. After all, you haven't invested large amounts of time or money into the endeavor yet, so you will not sustain any sizeable losses should you choose to abandon your Twitter campaign and look for marketing and sales solutions elsewhere. Naturally, it might prove difficult to step away from Twitter at this time, since it offers you and your business free and easy access to a huge audience of potential friends and clients. However, it is not too late to do so, should that be the right decision for you and your business.

- **Keep your ears open to the insights that the Twitterverse so freely offers.** You should know by this point in your evaluation of Twitter if you truly are interested in reading the tweets of those you follow and those who follow you. Have you been attentive to the tweets of others? Have you been able to extract valuable information from the trends, ideas, and even beliefs that others are tweeting about? While you shouldn't turn Twitter into any sort of armchair psychoanalysis, you should determine if you are willing to faithfully sort through and apply the thoughts and meanings behind other users' tweets to your business or brand. Do you intend to use the thoughts and opinions of others to help you establish and drive the philosophy of your business or brand—even if the Twitterverse thinks you're approaching your business in entirely the wrong way? If you are confronted with negative feedback, dig deeper to understand opposing viewpoints and determine whether you should incorporate those opinions into your overall business outreach strategy.

- **Ensure you've selected the Twitter user name that best represents your brand or business.** If you haven't already done so, you need to create a Twitter account that best represents your business or brand. As you will read in Part 4 of this book, several businesses and organizations have created successful user names by adding an identifier that explains why others should follow them onto the name of their company or organization (such as with the Twitter user names ComcastCares and AmazonDeals). If the user name you'd prefer is not available, quickly decide upon another and then work to establish it as the *real* face and voice of your company. Since registration is limited to only one Twitter account per real e-mail address, you'll need to be creative if your first choice has already been taken.

With that, it's time to commit to an engaging Twitter presence for your brand or business, if you haven't done so already. Even after you've finished reading this book, you should continually revisit your foundational purpose for creating a Twitter presence for your business, lest you stray off-message or forget why you're tweeting in the first place. Your Twitter strategy can and should evolve as you grow more comfortable with tweeting, but be certain that you always remain "on message."

▪▪▪▪ Being Engaging in Your Approach

If you're going to adopt Twitter for the long haul, you must continually strive to engage your followers and those whom you follow in a way that both supports traditional business-customer interactions and respects the interpersonal tone of Twitter. When you do so, you not only demonstrate to your fellow users that you value and respect the Twitterverse and those who make intelligent use of it; you also set yourself apart as a business, brand, or individual who wants to get more and *give more* on Twitter. If you find that your engagement skills need some polishing, consider applying one or more of the following tactics to your tweeting:

- **Instead of only telling your followers what you are *doing*, sometimes tell them what you're *seeing*, *reading*, *hearing*, or *thinking*.** Whatever it is that has your attention, use it to open up an appropriate interaction that isn't necessarily focused on your business or product but rather on a topic or idea into which your followers might have some input. In doing so, you can provide deeper access to who you are (or who your brand or company is) while learning more about who your followers are.

- **When you tweet links to your business website or blog, be sure to preface the URL with a compelling and concise statement that explains where the link leads and why your followers might be interested in clicking on it.** Even if your followers decide against clicking through to your link, they will be appreciative that you respected their time enough to provide them with a brief summary of the linked content so that they could assess whether or not they wanted to navigate forward.

- **Take the time to frequently ask your followers questions.** After all, the art of Twitter engagement involves enticing your followers to actively and freely provide *their* input. If your tweets remain in "tell" mode, you might as well publish a closed blog where you can offer your perceptions—and yours alone—on whatever it is that you're interested in. When you open up the conversation, however, you gain involvement from your followers and attract them to you, your business, or your brand.

- **Don't forget to retweet interesting updates to your followers that have been posted by the people *you* follow.** Remember, Twitter relationships are communal by nature, so it stands to reason that your followers will be appreciative when you bring attention-grabbing or otherwise useful tweets from another user to their attention. While you should take care to maintain your focus on *your* tweets and *your* business, you also should selectively retweet updates that are complementary to that which you tweet about.

- **Consider sharing your company's tweeting responsibility with your business partner or fellow teammates.** As long as each tweeter has a firm understanding of your company's identity and is committed to upholding and protecting the core essence of your business, your company will benefit from acquainting its followers with the various individuals that help produce their favorite product. So, open your company's doors and humanize your business by letting your followers get to know the people that keep your company or brand ticking.

Engagement is an art—it really is. If you want to forge truly successful interpersonal relationships with your followers and customers, approach them honestly and genuinely. When you do so, your followers will recognize that you are trustworthy and forthright, which will give your business an edge over competitors that only engage potential customers from a rigid business-customer mindset. So, adapt to this new way of interacting with your customers and you will be in the best position possible to reach and exceed your business goals.

■ ■ ■ Engaging Confidently by Applying the Unwritten Rules of "Twittiquette"

You probably have been wondering if there is an accepted protocol or code of conduct to which tweeters adhere. Well, while there are no official rules of engagement (save for the actual site rules you read about in Chapter 2), users do generally agree to follow a somewhat loose set of tweeting guidelines that was established by the Twitter community itself. Of course, nobody has stepped forward to claim the official title of Mr. or Ms. Manners of the social media realm, but Twitter users do engage with one another according to the following tenets of good tweeting, which you also will be expected to uphold:

■ **Keep your tweet short and sweet.** Pardon the rhyme, but your followers expect you to get to the point quickly and clearly. If your tweets are long and rambling, your followers will most likely lose interest in what you have to say. Consider each tweet, construct it thoughtfully, and remember that unless you are sending a direct message, *everyone* can read your Twitter posts.

- **Don't fill up on tweets.** Pace your tweets, and remember, if you tweet incessantly, those who follow you will not be happy to find their own Twitter home pages filled with nothing more than your barrage of messages. If you have a lot to tweet about, consider publishing a blog and tweet only to inform your followers that a new entry has been posted. Otherwise, let someone else get a word in edgewise—literally.

- **Be reasonable in the number of people you follow.** While there are plenty of interesting tweeters out there, it's hardly conceivable that you could derive value from or be valuable to any more than two or three hundred Twitter users. If your Twitter profile reveals that you're following hundreds or thousands of people, other users might think you're a spammer who has established an account for the sole purpose of amassing a large number of followers to assail with an onslaught of spammy tweets. Focus on demonstrating to the Twitterverse that you're truly selective about those you follow, and you'll stand a better chance of projecting the image that you're worth following, too.

- **Work to deliver a complete and self-contained tweet in a single message.** While you can develop a progressive message over the course of several tweets on occasion to mix up your tweet stream, remember that responses from your followers might interrupt your successive tweets, making it difficult for others to piece together your original post. Therefore, as a general rule, keep your message contained to a single tweet.

- **Don't attempt to follow *every* person who follows you.** While reciprocal following is encouraged, be sure that you are truly interested in the posts of the follower you're eyeing. When you carefully elect to follow only those users that have something of interest to add to the conversation, you also help your followers determine which Twitter users will infuse the most value into their tweet streams.

- **If you receive feedback that indicates that your posts are scattered, difficult to follow, or even spammy, be sure to listen and respond appropriately.** Here is where the customers will be indicating how well (or not so well) you're doing in your interaction. Pay careful attention to what they're telling you. If you ignore their feedback, they very well could ignore you, in turn.

These are just a few of the key etiquette points that govern Twitter and, as mentioned, they aren't "official" by any means. However, let the preceding tenets guide you in your efforts to make the most of Twitter for both yourself and those who follow you. Finally, remain attentive as you navigate your way through Twitter, and if you hear about or observe other social media manners worth heeding, be sure to do so!

■■■ Last Point: You Must Give Before You Can Receive

Now that you better understand the art of refined engagement on Twitter, we'll wrap up this chapter with a twist on the old maxim "'Tis better to give than to receive." We won't call that old adage into question here, but when it comes to socializing and engaging others on Twitter, the phrase "'Tis best to give before you attempt to receive" is more applicable. What's the difference, you ask? Well, as you recall, when you engage your audience and enlist your followers to help you spread the word about your business or your brand, you are actively asking them to do you a favor. Similarly, when you request that your followers click on the URLs you embed into your tweets and involve them in conversations that ultimately will help your business or brand thrive, you again are actively asking them to do you a favor. Now, it is fine to ask your followers to become your customers and proxy messengers—but not before you have established a foundation of trust and a history of interaction with them. So, how do you lay the groundwork for mutually beneficial Twitter relationships? You must first give something to your followers and only then ask for something in return.

When you first join Twitter, let other users know you've arrived by offering up information that's of interest or use to them, which serves as your first "give." See how they respond—as well as *if* they respond—and continue to speak to them on their terms until they get to know you. In doing so, you're acclimatizing to their realm, working to fit into their expectations, and offering up your second "give." As you engage your followers, let them know what you can offer them and help them find out more about your product, brand, or business on their own time. When you extend information to your followers in this pressure-free way, you are presenting them with your third "give." If and when they ask for more details on what you're offering, you can engage them more directly—and even grant them an introductory price or promotion on your products or services, which is yet another "give."

After you have converted your followers into transacting customers, you'll wonder if it's time to ask for a favor . . . but not yet. Let them absorb their experience with your product or service, and give them time to assess their interactions with you. Follow up with them to see if they are satisfied with your business or if there is anything further you can do to ensure that they're fully pleased, which stands as still another "give." When your customers indicate their satisfaction, you can then ask for a "receive" for yourself and inquire as to whether they would consider telling a friend or two about your products or services.

If you worry that the foregoing exercise was nothing more than a how-to lesson on customer manipulation, you can put any such misgivings behind you. In fact, the technique I just outlined for you is a very submissive business approach, and some companies might even claim that it is too passive to use in any real business situation. What those companies forget, however, is that the rules of customer engagement are very different in the realm of social media—especially on Twitter, where the conversation can turn very personal and personable. In this sense, Twitter ups the ante when it comes to genuinely engaging customers, but smart businesses will take advantage of the opportunities the social space presents them.

So, what else can you give before you hope to receive? Here's a quick list of "gives" you can offer up in the Twitter neighborhood:

- **Tweet help, advice, or guidance.** If your business delivers products or services that often generate customer questions, scan Twitter for those queries and dole out guidance as appropriate. Your business or service will credential you to provide assistance, and it also can serve as your calling card if and when those in the Twitterverse require additional support.

- **Offer your followers additional information that is relevant to the products or services you are marketing.** Encourage them to freely sample your wares and make it easy for them to share your informative messaging with those to whom it may be of use by embedding a link to an in-depth article or blog entry related to the topic at hand.

- **Extend promotions, discounts, and giveaways to your followers so they can safely sample your products without an immediate monetary commitment.** Allowing your followers to "test drive" your products before they buy them will prove that you are confident about what you offer.

- **Let your Twitter home page serve as an open venue where your followers can directly interact with you.** Sure, you could opt to engage your followers simply by tweeting updates, but why not show them how generous you are with your time and attention by connecting with them one-on-one? Time is not free, but if you spend it wisely with your customers, it will surely pay dividends.

As you can see, engagement is critical to business success—especially within the realm of Twitter. So, if you're ready to spread the word about your business or brand, approach Twitter in a manner that is social first, business-focused second, and interactive always. When you engage the Twitterverse respectfully, are a good steward of its underlying philosophy of free and open sharing and discussion, and give what you can to your followers, you may just find that your business receives more back from Twitter than you ever thought possible.

14

Gaining Advantage from
Twitter Advertising

"We leave the door open for advertising. We'd like to keep our options open, as we've said before."

—TWITTER FOUNDER BIZ STONE, AS POSTED ON TWITTER'S OFFICIAL BLOG

YOU ARE READING THIS book to focus on how you and your business can make money using Twitter, so I'm sure you understand why Twitter itself is also looking for ways to turn a profit. Ever since the microblogging service was developed and launched in March 2006, it has remained absolutely free for users—which obviously is good. On the other hand, if Twitter can't find a way to become financially self-sustaining, it could turn out to be an expensive failure and close its virtual doors—which obviously would be bad. Take heart, though, because the folks at Twitter understand the importance of generating revenue from their site and have begun to consider ways to incorporate advertising into their well-proven recipe for launching, growing, and firmly establishing a service that users simply cannot live without. While you might be concerned that Twitter will become just the latest Web service to succumb to an overwhelming amount of advertising that will muddle the user experience, read on to see how Twitter's decision to bring in advertising dollars could earn you extra revenue, too.

■ ■ ■ The Advent of Advertising on Twitter

On September 10, 2009, Twitter announced a revision to its terms of service agreement that stated the company's intention to pursue the inclusion of paid advertising content. That change reads as follows:

> The services may include advertisements, which may be targeted to the content or information on the services, queries made through the services, or other information. The types and extent of advertising by Twitter on the services are subject to change.
>
> In consideration for Twitter granting you access to and use of the services, you agree that Twitter and its third-party providers and partners may place such advertising on the services.

While announcements like these, which adjust the ad-free principle upon which many social networking services initially are based, often infuriate the more "organically minded" of Web users, many industry analysts and tech bloggers wondered why Twitter took so long to welcome advertising to its wildly popular site. Twitter's growth was phenomenal in its infancy, and thanks to significant infusions of venture capital, the site was able to avoid establishing a revenue-generating plan until recently. But the reality is that no website can subsist forever on the goodwill of venture capitalists. Twitter needs to create an income stream, and aside from charging its users for their use of the social networking tool, there is no other way for Twitter to generate revenue than by allowing advertising onto its site.

Despite what detractors may say, advertising on Twitter is a good move—assuming the site is able to seamlessly integrate ad content into Twitter's existing platform in a way that allows users to continue tweeting as they always have. Of course, this might not be a safe assumption at this time, given that cofounder Biz Stone himself has admitted that the company is nervous that ad content will only annoy

Twitter's user base. Stone once stated that the addition of banner ads on the site was "probably the least interesting thing we could do," and true to Twitter's favorable reputation of being eternally attentive to its discerning users, he also revealed that he is open to suggestions as to the best way to blend business with Twitter. At the time of this writing, no details about Twitter advertising content are set in stone, but rest assured that the site will listen to the concerns of its users and make adjustments to its advertising strategy accordingly.

▪▪▪ How Might Twitter Advertising Look?

The conundrum at hand at this moment regards how advertising can be gracefully squeezed into Twitter's very low-key style. Indeed, since the site's popularity largely has been based upon how easy it is to construct and consume tweets on computers via compact widgets (synonymous with "apps" for web pages—small functional elements that enable enhanced capabilities or convenience methods) and from handheld devices, a cluttering of glaring and blaring ad muck will surely cook this goose. Beyond this, some potential advertisers have indicated their initial reluctance to have their products and brands advertised within tweet streams that might include unexpected, unfiltered, and possibly offensive user-generated content.

Even so, the risk could well be worth the reward, as advertisers will be able to access and present their brands to the millions of "everywhere" users via targeted (that is, smart) relevancy placements; it's practically money in the bank! Considering how quickly Twitter has grown, how eagerly it has been adopted by the public, and how readily it has been infused into popular culture, the site's soil is fertile for consumer cultivating—if advertisers approach it carefully, that is.

When it comes to the careful cultivation of consumers, most agree that the best method of advertising on Twitter would be the sort that is barely noticeable. What's that, you say? If it's barely noticeable, why bother? Here's why: as opposed to the annoying, bombastic, in-your-face fly-out ads you typically find online—that is, they find you and interrupt your surfing with pop-up ads whose "close" buttons are more difficult to find than Waldo among a sea of beachcombers—subtle advertising occurs organically within a stream of discussion and doesn't interfere with users' Web-browsing experience. It also just so happens to be one of the most effective forms of advertising.

The term that is being used to refer to these more subtle ads is "in-stream" advertising, which implies that "ad tweets" would be inserted into already in-progress tweet streams. Using keyword detection and user preference tracking, advertisers could develop non-intrusive tweets that lead followers to a product, service, or other such offering that is congruent with the discussion at hand. So, if Twitterers are chatting about a particular band or recording artist, Apple iTunes could insert an ad tweet into the tweet stream with a link to that particular band or recording artist's iTunes store. Those who follow the link could then purchase songs and video content from the artist's iTunes store without disrupting the flow of messaging. As long as they are not inserted into tweet streams too often (a detail that would need to be worked out among Twitter, advertisers, and ideally actual users), ad tweets could even infuse additional value into users' Twitter experience. If you fear that the slow introduction of advertising to Twitter will assuredly create an onslaught of merchandising mess, consider how this transition could actually engage consumers even more—provided Twitter has the courage and mettle to keep the plaid-jacket bunch at bay:

- **If Twitter account holders are free to opt into including advertising content within their tweet streams, then they will be able to select the types of products and services that are relevant to their followers.** As such, folks hosting business-centric Twitter accounts can provide recommendations to their followers, likely with converted link-to-purchase transactions earning the referrer some form of compensation (the old affiliate method). By this methodology, tweeters will need to use their discretion when determining the number of ad tweets to opt into, since if they select too many, they will likely annoy and lose their audience.

- **If Twitter gives the green light to targeted advertising, an ad bot could read and interpret the keywords and hashtags that account holders insert into their tweets and intersperse relevant ads into users' tweet streams in a meaningful yet unobtrusive way.** This is truly significant, since if Twitter goes this route, then account holders can literally assert the sorts of products they *want* advertised within their tweet streams. In this way, account holders can maintain control of their ad content and effectively further deliver value to their followers by enabling ad content that is useful to those who monitor their tweets. Naturally, this method surely wouldn't be error-free, and it's likely that the Twitter team and its advertising partners would need to remain ever-vigilant to assure the ad algorithms don't accidentally place advertisements for Victoria's Secret lingerie amid a discussion on dairy farming.

Again, don't expect that Twitter's adoption of ad content will be trouble- and tweak-free. However, if we can hold Biz Stone to his word that he is open-minded and willing to make adjustments to Twitter's ad strategy as the need arises, then it's likely that Twitter will manage this change deftly. And through it all, you, the business-minded tweeter, stand to benefit.

Of course, you don't *have* to wait for Twitter's forthcoming adoption of ad content to begin applying some astute advertising techniques of your own to your tweet stream.

■■■ Beginning Your Own In-Stream Advertising Campaign

By this point in our discussion on advertising, you might be asking yourself, "Hey, why can't I begin interspersing advertisements into my tweet stream myself?" Know what? You can. Although your primary usage of Twitter should always be to engage your audience (customers) with relevant but not overly promotional messaging, you can begin injecting advertisements into your tweet stream right away—if you are careful.

Previously in this book, you were encouraged to develop and post your tweets carefully to ensure that they are useful, meaningful, and of value to your followers. The same holds true when it comes to carefully planning and plotting your advertising efforts, too. The good news is that advertising via your tweet stream *can* be done, and when it is done right, your followers will likely be thankful that you've brought a particular product or service to their audience's attention.

How will you be able to proceed confidently in this endeavor by your own efforts? Here's how:

- **Keep the advertisement relevant to your tweet stream.** Yes, this has been said previously in this chapter, but it bears repeating because it is tantamount to your advertising success on Twitter.
- **Clearly identify the ad post as what it is—an ad.** Consider starting the message with "ADV:" or "Ad:" so that your followers will recognize the message as advertisement. Why? Remember that Twitter is based on honesty and clarity. Scant few will begrudge you for popping in an ad from time to time, since the vast majority of users recognize that a business needs to make money to remain solvent. When you insert the "ad flag" into your ad tweets, you help your followers easily see which messages are sales-related and, in doing so, show your respectful engagement with your audience.
- **Tweet your ad message several times over the course of the day to ensure that the majority of your followers see it.** Remember, it's to your benefit to expose as many people as possible to the ad. Provided you have an active tweet stream, tweet the ad three times a day for no more than three days in any given seven-day stretch for best results. You're free and encouraged to modify these guidelines if you're gaining improved response from your followers, but I urge you to start out cautiously.

Now that you understand some key ad-tweet guidelines, read through the following list of precautions to get a better idea of what to avoid when you engage in active advertising within your tweet stream:

- **Don't tweet too many ads, nor should you tweet any one ad too often.** Remember, tweeting should be about healthily and respectfully engaging with your followers. No one wants to be beat over the head with incessant advertising. As a general rule, consider limiting the appearance rate of your ads so that they are tweeted no more than once for every twenty-five to thirty tweets.
- **Don't allow the ads to become "buzzkills."** If the dialogue is flowing fluidly between you and your followers, don't unceremoniously stymie the conversation's natural momentum with the Twitter equivalent of "And now a word from our sponsor." Craft ad tweets as cleverly as you craft your regular messages. Try to make your ad messages fun, upbeat, and even entertaining, and insert them only at appropriate moments within the dialogue.
- **Avoid using third-party ad-insertion services.** There are several sites that have emerged of late that promise to help you effectively monetize your Twitter activity if you allow *them* to monitor and insert ads within your tweet stream. Generally, teaming up with these third-party ad-insertion services is a bad idea—unless, of course, you find one that is willing to give you active engagement and control over the ad content before any ad is inserted. Typically, though, these third-party services cannot give the focused attention to your business methods and interactions in the same way that you can—and that your followers have come to expect from you. For this reason, be wary of turning over the keys to another ad-insertion service. Instead, work with Twitter's on-site advertising function when it is launched and ready to use.
- **Don't forget your promise to your followers.** Remember, you are on Twitter in order to talk to your audience, your customers, in a way that you yourself would like to be engaged. Do unto them as you would like to have done unto you. If you are consider-

ing posting an ad or ad stream that is annoying to you, it certainly will be annoying to your followers. If you find yourself agonizing over whether or not to unleash a particular ad or ad stream upon your followers, chances are you've already received your answer; don't do it. Don't abuse your followers with any content of any kind that is even remotely obnoxious.

Because Twitter offers a method of outreach and connection that previously was not available, it makes sense that businesses and individuals alike are harnessing the tool to generate revenue through advertising. However, if you choose to implement an advertising strategy on Twitter, proceed with caution and at all times incorporate skill and smart thinking into your advertising outreach efforts. When you perpetually consider how your followers might react to advertising content—that is, products and services that are now endorsed by you—within your tweet stream, you will maintain the clarity of purpose, vision, and responsibility to do what's best for your customers and your business.

15

Ten Microblogging Mistakes to Avoid

Up to this point, this book has guided you through the best ways to utilize Twitter for your business or brand and stressed those strategies you should leverage to get the most out of your efforts. In this chapter, however, a cautionary finger will be raised and explicitly pointed at certain things you shouldn't do when engaging in microblogging activities. As you read through this list of microblogging miscues to avoid, you will discover that the preferred alternate course of action for each misstep has already been laid out for you in a previous chapter.

Take heed, then, and be certain to watch out for and avoid these ten all-too-common mistakes of microblogging.

1. Lack of a Plan

For some folks, "failure to launch" is not the problem. No, the problem is failing to plan where to go after launching. You may have diligently set goals and determined a means to achieve them (product or service announcements, promotions, and so on). However, if you failed to set milestones to ensure that you are constantly making forward progress or, more important, have not been using these checkpoints to determine if a course correction is needed, you may wander off into the ether, unsure of where you're going. Sure, creating a plan can be boring to some. After all, the nuts and bolts of reaching a target often are less than riveting, and many people would rather spend their mindshare in more creative and expressive realms. That's fine, but unless you know for certain that your passion is well guided and will ultimately return dividends, you're just another "yakker" in the mix. Don't let a lack of planning derail your aspirations. Sharpen your pencil, gain some focus, and get a plan down on paper before you get too carried away in your quest. And, yes, you'll need to revisit your plan frequently—at least every one to three months after you've soundly launched—to track your progress and plan your next target.

■■■ 2. Fuzzy Focus

Do you recall the strong encouragement I gave you in Part 1 of this book to be sure not only of your intent in tweeting but also of Twitter's applicability to your brand or business? Believe it or not, even those with the best-laid Twitter plan sometimes veer off-course into ambiguity, and their tweeting goes from focused to fuzzy. If this happens to you, flip back to Chapter 4's discussion of tweet timing and ensure that your tweets remain on key. By utilizing a bit of a formulaic approach, you will be able to maintain your focus and still remain appropriately engaging—and even spontaneous—over the course of a day or week.

■■■ 3. Forgetting to Promote

Regardless of size, some businesses become overly concerned that their followers perceive their tweets as perpetual pitches, so they unwittingly stop pitching altogether. But if a company doesn't pitch its services or products with appropriate regularity, how will its followers know if it is still in business at all? To avoid this scenario, make sure that your tweet plan includes "pitch points"—or predetermined moments in your tweeting schedule when you will set up and then launch pitches within your tweet stream. Keep your intent for tweeting in focus, as it will remind you that you're on Twitter first and foremost to promote a product, service, or brand.

■■■ 4. Unrealistic Expectations

Having unrealistic expectations about your results on Twitter is likely the most difficult microblogging mistake to avoid falling victim to. Naturally, each of us fantasizes that upon launch of our Twitter account, the Twitterverse will crowd our page, excitedly buzzing, "What took you so long to get here? We've been so eager for you to arrive." Sure, we are all hopeful that thousands of folks will be scanning for tweets like ours and will find the experience of following us to be refreshing and rewarding. In reality, however, it usually takes a while to get noticed, establish a solid identity, and attract reliable followers. Patience is an essential aspect of any good Twitter plan, so if it's not already included in yours, add it in now. Take your first month on Twitter to get used to tweeting and following those whose tweets are interesting or relevant to your business. The activity on your Twitter page will pick up eventually, but you won't become a Twitter success overnight. Trust that taking a slow and steady approach to Twitter will garner you the best sort of followers and allow you the time you need to hone your style. Again, practice patience at the outset and you'll avoid feeling let down just as you're beginning.

■■■ 5. Distracted by Details

Sometimes Twitter users can become so engrossed in planning out their tweeting strategies and fleshing out the details of their Twitter personas that they neglect to post tweets that are content-rich and engaging. Ever wonder why your Twitter home page only allows for limited customization? It's so that you can get down to tweeting practically immediately! While you certainly want to spend a decent amount of time developing a catchy and compelling brand and style for yourself on Twitter, you want to be sure you're not trying to gold-plate a plastic cup. Put another way, engaging the Twitterverse and completing your start-up learning curve should be your first priorities, not tinkering with and tweaking your profile image, background, color scheme, and user name. Be aware that this sort of ongoing detailing is sometimes a cover for procrastination. If you find yourself falling prey to procrastinating your tweeting, honestly ask yourself what's keeping you from jumping in.

■■■6. Too Much Reading

While some Twitter users agonize over detailing their Twitter home-pages to avoid tweeting, others get so caught up in reading other users' tweet streams (or blogs or websites) that they never get around to managing their own Twitter presences. While it is important that you spend some time each day reading your followers' tweets and keeping regular tabs on your particular area of interest or industry, don't make doing so an open-ended event. Instead, allow yourself to spend a limited amount of time each day reading others' tweets. If you like to start the day by checking up Twitterverse trends, take thirty to sixty minutes before you start tweeting to do just that. If, on the other hand, you're more productive when you start your stream of tweeting the moment you begin your day, then resolve to avoid reading what others are up to until you've gotten your initial "work" done. Whatever your schedule, limit the amount of time you spend surfing the content of others. Otherwise, you will risk slipping into their streams of consciousness while your followers are left to wonder if you've lapsed into unconsciousness.

■■■7. Lack of Interesting Content

This particular misstep is certainly not intended to criticize or pass judgment on your writing, but frankly, you have to be sure you're offering up content that is interesting and engaging to your followers. If your business is all about rubber gaskets, you might be challenged to draw a crowd at a cocktail party. Then again, if you can spice up the conversation by dangling an intriguing premise, you'd be surprised. Rather than blandly posit, "If you want to save water and money, you should replace your toilet tank gaskets," why not tweet something along the lines of "I heard my toilet gag last night, swallowing another wad of cash"? You get the idea. Get creative if you're not convinced that the product or service you're pitching will stop them in their tracks. Use a twist of phrase, appropriate humor, and even a bit of mystery in your posts to get the ball rolling.

■■■8. Lack of Engagement

Some folks are just naturally talented at engaging those they come into contact with, while others must actively and diligently work toward being engaging. Regardless of which camp you fall into, you must learn to speak the language of engagement if you want to get the most from your Twitter experience. Spend some time observing how those you follow engage their audiences and see if you're able to replicate their strategy. Be genuine, of course, but be sure you tweet in a way that encourages your followers to chime in. Remember to ask questions, post surveys, allow conversation, and properly time your responses to keep the conversation alive and lively. You needn't have been born a social butterfly to be engaging; you just need to keep the door open—and keep opening it—to encourage others to enter the conversation.

■ ■ ■ 9. Striving for Perfection

Try to stay realistic: Not every one of your tweets will sound like it was typed by Hemingway, Thurber, or King—and that's OK. After all, there is no such thing as the "perfect tweet." With this in mind, avoid growing overwhelmed by the feeling that every word in every tweet needs to be carefully screened and selected. Sure, your tweets should be consistent with the style and intent that you originally set forth for your Twitter presence, but there is no need to belabor every single post. In fact, agonizing over a 140-character utterance will not only put the friendly and engaging style that your followers have come to expect in jeopardy, but it also will be a colossal waste of time. Your tweets might be a bit clumsy at the start, but you'll develop a style and rhythm for your messaging that upholds your Twitter philosophy and successfully engages new and old followers alike. Trust yourself and your tweeting style. If you get caught up in second-guessing yourself, no one—not you, not your followers, and certainly not your brand or business—will get anything out of your tweets.

■ ■ ■ 10. Failure to Enjoy

Above all else, avoid turning your tweeting into drudgery. This is a fun and interactive opportunity for you to connect with other people. Think of Twitter as the virtual equivalent of the Cheers bar in Boston, the one made famous in the 1980s sitcom of the same name. Patrons frequented Cheers because it was a fun place that offered camaraderie over consumerism. The conversation was quick, often pointed, and intentionally witty, but the charm of the setting is what drew people in and, since they were at a bar, why not order a drink or two? Similarly, if you establish a fun and welcoming setting of sorts at your Twitter home page, the rest will fall into place. If you don't truly enjoy tweeting, your lack of enthusiasm will ring through in your tweets, and your followers will discover that they are fairly lackluster about your tweets, too.

Many of the items on this list are rooted in common sense, but the truth is that they are the some of the most common mistakes made by people who otherwise have perfectly sound and reasonable intentions for microblogging. Perhaps the very reason that these mistakes are made so frequently is because they're tossed aside as, "Well, everyone knows that." However, what we know and what we do are often two very different things. As you're readying now to dive into your tweeting at full throttle, just remain aware of these common missteps and be sure to avoid them whenever and wherever possible.

16

Other Microblogging Boosters

As the preceding chapters of this book have made clear, Twitter is only the tip of the social iceberg; it's a conversation starter and an easy-to-digest discussion feed, but it's not the full story. In some ways, Twitter is that ear-catching statement you overhear in a social setting that draws you to the spot where the topic is being further discussed or debated. That said, Twitter is not a stand-alone solution for boosting your business or brand but rather is just one of many ways to draw attention to what you have to offer. With that, following are some additional sites and tools that you should employ along with Twitter to develop and deliver a well-rounded online representation of you and your business.

■ ■ ■ Blogging: Blogger.com or WordPress

The terms "blog" and "blogging" have cropped up several times over the course of this book, so it should come as no surprise that I'd encourage you to start up a blog of your own—if you haven't already done so. Why blog when you are already microblogging, you ask? Well, as you assuredly know by now, there is quite literally only so much can say when you microblog. When it comes to spreading the news about your product, service, or brand, microblogs function in much the same way that colorful announcements painted on the windshields of used cars do. Indeed, just as windshield proclamations of "nice and clean," "low miles," and "drive me home today" are meant to act as headlines and eye-catchers that cause passersby to pause a moment, microblogs are attention-getters that hint at an underlying value to reading the information they contain. However, just as drivers cannot be certain that they want to purchase a car if they never peer inside the window, open the door, and take the vehicle for a test drive, your potential customers won't be fully sold on you or your business if you don't provide them with a more detailed, fleshed-out look at your products, services, or brand.

Therefore, you'll want to host a blog that provides your customers with the details, the fulfillment of your promises, and the value behind what you tweet. With a blog, you can relay far more information about what you offer than you would be able to over the course of many, many tweets. The two most popular blogging services at this time are Blogger.com and WordPress.com, so decide which is to your liking and get blogging (see Figure 16-1).

Figure 16-1. Blogger.com (http://blogger.com) and Wordpress (http://wordpress.com) are two popular blogging services that allow users to create a blog and then begin posting updates to it in no time at all.

▪▪▪ LinkedIn

LinkedIn has been a fixture in the social media stratosphere for several years now and remains a stable site and platform for engaging other business-minded folks, sharing ideas, connecting and collaborating with industry peers and associates, and generally keeping tabs on what's rising over the business horizon. The frequently trafficked and highly regarded site gives its high-caliber associates access to a bona fide network of professionals, who are often of significant help

Figure 16-2. Access an unparalleled network of business professionals at LinkedIn. Go to http://linkedin.com to learn more and register.

to one another. Registration and use of LinkedIn is highly recommended for businesspeople like you (see Figure 16-2).

▪▪▪Digg

This "social content" site allows users to submit articles, blog postings, and other bits of online content to the Digg community to see whether their fellow members *digg* their submissions or not. So, why not submit your business's blog or one of your new products for digging? If the community diggs your submission, your content and your brand are promoted on the website and recommended to other users to digg, too. It's best if an already-respected Digg user posts a link to your content, but you can also do so yourself. If you choose the latter route, keep your fingers crossed that other users find your submission and decide to digg it, because enough diggs might just cause your content, service, or brand to go viral. So, give some attention to Digg, which has the potential to expose your brand to plenty of eyeballs without a lot of work and at virtually no expense (see Figure 16-3).

Figure 16-3. Digg is the place to go to expose your content, service, or brand to a vast online community of viewers and reviewers. Visit http://digg.com for all the details.

■ ■ ■ StumbleUpon

On the surface, StumbleUpon might appear to be yet another online time sink, but it actually is a wildly popular hybrid of search engine and social networking site (see Figure 16-4). At StumbleUpon, users download an innocuous toolbar into which they can enter search terms for the type of content they are looking for. Then, upon clicking the button labeled "Stumble," StumbleUpon takes users on a tour of thousands of user-recommended sites that match their query. The StumbleUpon community rates sites with a "thumbs up" or a "thumbs down" and, in doing so, positions them within the stream of useful and interesting Web destinations that are served up in response to a user's search. Naturally, you'll want to StumbleUpon your own site or blog and give it an initial "thumbs up" so that it is added to the StumbleUpon Web stream for consideration by the rest of the community. After that, let the community do its work to gain you increased visibility while you tend to your business. It's simple, fun, and it yields results.

Figure 16-4. Visit StumbleUpon at http://stumbleupon.com and submit your site to a community of users that will help you gain exposure while you tend to other things.

■■■ Flickr

If you haven't already done so, now is the time to visit Flickr at http://flickr.com, the online destination where amateur and professional photographers alike convene to upload their images and browse through those of other Flickr users (see Figure 16-5). From a business perspective, Flickr is the perfect place to host a gallery of your product images, original creations, projects in development, and more. Not only does the site create unique URLs for each image you upload (to embed in compressed format when you tweet), but its community of users is constantly on the prowl and searches through and comments on all the images its fellow users upload. Who knows? Maybe some Flickr users will happen upon your content even when you're not minding your photo stream!

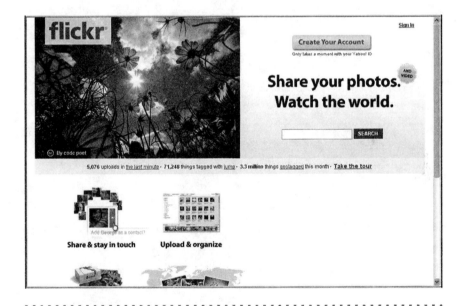

Figure 16-5. Flickr puts images of your products and brand within easy reach of not only you, but also other Flickr users, who actively pore through the site's content in search of new and exciting images at http://flickr.com.

■ ■ ■ ■ ■ ■ ■ ■ ■ ■ ■ ■ ■ ■ ■ ■ ■ ■

PART 4

Look, Listen, and Learn: Twitter Success Stories

By this point, you should have a solid understanding of how Twitter can add a new dimension to your business activity and results. You've learned about the business need that motivated Jack Dorsey to invent Twitter, you've realized how quickly Twitter has caught on with plugged-in individuals, and you've discovered how the seemingly simple Twitter toolset can grant you unprecedented access to your customers—and vice versa.

If, for whatever reason, you *still* are not yet fully convinced that Twitter is the right social media tool for you and your business, then seeing is definite cause for believing. In this special section of the book, you'll read about actual businesses and services that are leveraging Twitter to their advantage. You likely will be familiar with some of the businesses that are profiled in the following pages, while others may be new to you. All of them, however, have discovered how Twitter can improve their customer interactions, reinforce their customer service, and ultimately strengthen their brand. The tweets you will read in the following case studies are real, and the company representatives who are mentioned are actual people who are dedicated to bettering their businesses' relationship with their customers.

Read on, now, to see Twitter in business action. As you examine each case study, try to pinpoint parallels between each of the profiled businesses and your own. Note which elements of their Twitter strategies best suit your intended approach, and be sure to cite the businesses you take as inspiration in your own Twitter outreach plan.

17

Zappos.com
(http://twitter.com/zappos)

IF IT'S A PARTICULAR pair or style of shoes that you're seeking, there's a Kentucky warehouse that might have what you want. It's Zappos.com, the online shoe and fashion connection that carries more than a thousand brands and as many colors and styles, too. Around the clock, the Zappos.com warehouse is kicking it—literally—to fulfill customer orders from across the nation and around the globe. With an inventory that features millions of items, it has been rightly remarked that what Amazon.com did for books, Zappos .com is doing for shoes.

If you were to truly gaze into the inner workings at Zappos.com, however, you'd discover that this shoe company is not built on an always-on, always toiling workforce that is constantly seeking the largest bottom line among its competitors. Rather, Zappos.com is a company that prides itself on the high premium it places on maintaining an enjoyable working environment. After all, as Zappos.com CEO and cofounder Tony Hsieh confirms, excellence cannot be drummed into a team through dogmatic mission statements. It must be inspired by a company's culture, which is exactly what Zappos.com does to great effect. Hsieh, a young entrepreneur who is clearly wise beyond his years, knows that a strong, supportive, and friendly family-like work culture will naturally—organically—breed pride in execution for every order received, to every customer's delight. Without a doubt, Hsieh is a man driven by philosophical pursuits, and he has been able to successfully apply his grounding principles to his business. Zappos .com survived the dot-com bust—the company has been in business since 1999 and continues to grow stronger every year—yet understands how its originating culture continues to inspire its employees to deliver an unrivaled customer experience.

So, what might Hsieh be tweeting about on the company's Twitter page, http://twitter.com/zappos (see Figure 17-1)? If you guessed

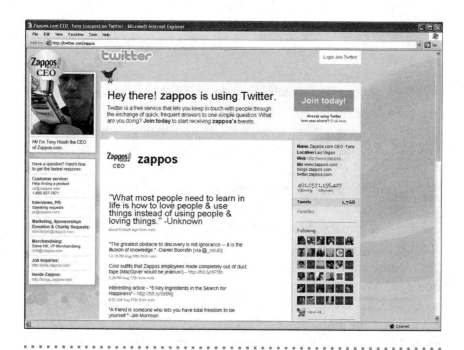

Figure 17-1. Find out what makes online success Zappos.com tick—from the heart and soul of its own CEO.

philosophy and observances that illuminate life's truths and para-doxes, you'd be right. When you become a follower of Hsieh's tweet stream, you'll be treated to the gamut of "what's it all about" proc-lamations and postulations. How is this appropriate to the Zappos .com business? Simply enough, Hsieh provides his followers with positive input through the philosophical and general interest tidbits he inserts into his tweets and, in doing so, underscores and upholds his company's core values. When followers read Hsieh's tweet stream, they gain a deeper view into the philosophy of Zappos.com and also become personally engaged with Hsieh himself. Therefore, Hsieh's tweet stream is engaging, maintains consistency with his company's identity, and enables customers to access the operational philosophy that drives Zappos.com. In this sense, Zappos.com's Twitter pres-ence is an excellent example of how the social networking tool can strengthen the ties between a business and its customers.

■ ■ ■ ■ ■ ■ ■ ■ ■ ■ ■ ■ ■ ■ ■ ■ ■

18

Berry Chill Yogurt Couture
(http://twitter.com/yogijones)

IT'S AN INDISPUTABLE FACT that Chicago-based Berry Chill has brought new a culture to the social media scene—literally. In 2008, then twenty-nine-year-old Michael Farah took a U-turn away from his profession as a crude-oil futures trader and elected to offer something more refined to the Chicagoland community, Berry Chill Yogurt Couture. After noticing that few existing "frozen yogurt" parlors offered chilled and creamy treats that actually contain the much-vaunted probiotics—you know, those microscopic active cultures that are said to naturally boost people's metabolism, improve their immune response, manage their cholesterol, and even eliminate bad breath—Farah launched his truly good-for-you snack shop in January of the same year and has gone on to open more stores in the Chicagoland area. Customer response has been as active and beneficial as the celebrated bacteria in Farah's product, making Berry Chill a hip hangout for healthy indulgences.

So what's Farah doing on Twitter? Actually, *he's* not doing anything; company mascot Yogi Jones is doing all of the tweeting—and he's doing it well (see Figure 18-1). Naturally, Yogi is keeping a well-paced stream of tweets that informs his followers of the day's flavors and broadcasts important company announcements, like one tweet that trumpeted Berry Chill's new curbside yogurt service. There are also plenty of freebies and discounts for loyal followers, but in order to take advantage of tweeted offers, Berry Chill cleverly requires claimants to show that they're actually Twitter followers of Yogi's stream. In this way, Yogi has created a fun and rewarding way to engage his followers and encourage them to help spread the word about Berry Chill's good stuff. Additionally, Yogi often will offer up concert tickets for local shows, provided responders retweet Yogi's updates to prove that they are actively following his tweet stream.

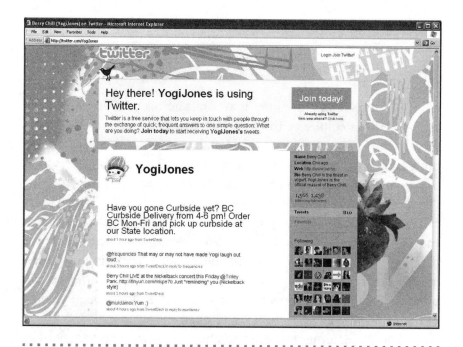

Figure 18-1. When you follow Yogi Jones, the tweeting voice of Berry Chill Yogurt Couture, you're in for some light and easy chat—and plenty of tempting treats.

If there's a risk to Berry Chill's Twitter approach, it's that the company's tweet stream is almost exclusively focused on promotion. While this type of Twitter strategy can elicit disdain from followers who prefer not to be pitched to in a nonstop fashion, Yogi manages to craft his tweets in a fun and friendly style. He also throws in plenty of giveaways to show his followers that their attention and patronage is nicely rewarded and always appreciated. Study Berry Chill's Twitter method for a crash course in promoting pleasantly by satisfying everyone's soft spot—the taste bud.

19

Naked Pizza
(http://twitter.com/nakedpizza)

SURE, "WORLD'S HEALTHIEST PIZZA" might slightly tug your interest, and the name might be worth looking at briefly if your gaze was already trained in that direction anyway. But Naked Pizza will flat out get you to stop in your tracks, turn around, and take a good, long look. Located in uptown New Orleans, newly rebranded Naked Pizza boasts the—you guessed it—world's healthiest pizza, which is made from all-natural ingredients, including prebiotic- and probiotic-infused multigrain crusts. And although the company has a firm following that is willing to spend upwards of one million dollars annually on its great-tasting and healthy pizza pies, Naked Pizza cofounder Jeff Leach has taken his messaging down the organic growth path.

Determined to shift his marketing expenses and efforts to the Twitterverse, Leach adopted Twitter as recently as spring 2009—and the gamble has paid off handsomely for Naked Pizza. During a one-day marketing blitz via tweets alone, Naked Pizza boasted that two-thirds of the day's lucrative business was derived from its 140-character message stream. In just four short months, Naked

Pizza has gathered nearly six thousand active followers, and according to Leach, these folks account for roughly 20 percent of the company's ongoing business. Because he is so satisfied with how easy Twitter has made it to engage, encourage, and entertain his customers, Leach has deleted the restaurant's landline phone information from Naked Pizza's website, http://www.nakedpizza.biz, opting instead to provide his customers with the company's Twitter URL. Of course, Naked Pizza maintains a solid Web presence, where customers can review nutrition information, peruse the menu, and make easy food orders online. The site even features an embedded YouTube video, which shows customers clamoring inside the restaurant, professing their love for Naked Pizza, and indicating that they have happily recommended the pies to their friends. Word-of-mouth advertising is truly at work in this land of guilt-free indulgence.

But are the pizza parlor's tweets engaging and effective, or is the Naked Pizza tweet stream merely a gimmick that exploits what some have called the "faddism" of Twitter? As a matter of fact, Leach and his team have aptly squeezed every drop of Naked Pizza's all-natural sauce into their Twitter presence, mixing up a clever blend of promotion and humor. Followers are regularly treated to sales, special offers, and coupon codes that can be applied to online orders, making it easy for customers to take advantage of the day's deal. Coincidentally, when Naked Pizza tweets about its promotional discounts, the company also makes it easy for its followers to forward the deals along to their family and friends, thereby increasing the likelihood that the messages will go viral. There's also some fun in Naked Pizza's lighthearted tweet stream. Take a look at some of Naked Pizza's recent tweets that demonstrate just how adept the pizza parlor is at interacting with its audience:

- 2 for 1 Tuesday. Great value. Online order code: TUES or 2 lrg 2 topping $19.95 (code: 2FOR20) http://www.nakedpizza.biz
- customer appreciation day! any lrg specialty $9.95 or lrg 1 topping $6.95. between 4-8 today only. no limit. 865-0244

- holy crap its raining!! i guess they don't call it a swamp for nothing. more coffee. stay home 2night & get pizza.
- free pizza for a month to anyone who can make it stop raining. proof of stoppage required.

By infusing humor into its tweets and commenting on the local weather, Naked Pizza expertly engages its followers, and although the pizza parlor's tweet stream features plenty of promotion, it does so in a way that is well-timed, value-oriented, rewarding, and entertaining for its audience (see Figure 19-1).

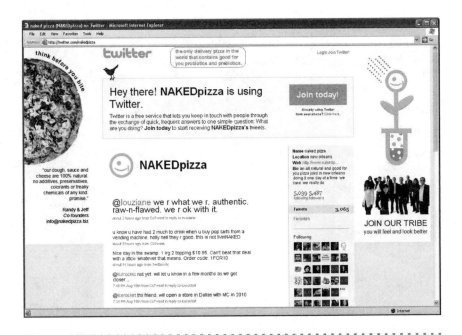

Figure 19-1. Don't avert your eyes—Naked Pizza is good for everyone, and the company has a firm handle on how to get the word out about its pies via Twitter.

20

Comcast
(http://twitter.com/comcastcares)

IF EVER YOU'VE LOOKED for an example of how word-of-mouth can all but destroy a company's image, look no further than Comcast, the cable and Internet provider that enjoys significant market share but is also burdened by a hefty public-perception problem. Comcast became the whipping post not only for its dissatisfied customers, who complained long and loud about the company's subpar performance and impossible-to-reach customer service representatives, but also for active bloggers and industry analysts, who lent a virtual bullhorn to disgruntled subscribers to ensure that their outrage could be heard in every corner of cyberspace. The cable and Internet provider was tarnished and troubled, and even though it was able to hold onto its sizeable market share, those who lived in locales that were only serviced by Comcast were less than pleased about their lack of options. It wasn't a good situation, and Comcast's reputation was growing worse each day.

Then came http://twitter.com/comcastcares, as well as an impassioned service director named Frank Eliason. His official title is Director of Digital Care, but unofficially he is the savior of the company's embattled persona. Because he knows how valuable—and important—searching the Twitterverse for mentions of his company is, Eliason has been able to address the unflattering sentiments about Comcast that swirl around Twitter and routinely asks unhappy tweeters, "Can I help?" By actively and passionately engaging those tweeters that are displeased with his company or its service, Eliason has been able to reverse the negative perception of Comcast and now is something of a Twitter star in his own right. He also has proved that effective use of Twitter can not only help companies and brands create a specific reputation for themselves—be it fun, helpful, results-oriented, or something else—it also can enable businesses with public perception problems to reverse the way they are regarded by others (see Figure 20-1).

Figure 20-1. When it comes to brand repair and meaningful customer assistance, Frank Eliason has become the face of Comcast on Twitter—literally, that's his face you see.

Since he first began directing Comcast's Twitter presence, Eliason has forged solid and friendly relationships with the company's customers and followers, some of whom he admits started the conversation by throwing down the gauntlet and declaring, "I don't like you." He has utilized social media to keep a brand from going bad and has effectively set the bar very high for other businesses that are using Twitter to engage their customers and clientele in an honest and caring manner. Thanks to Eliason, comcastcares has proven to be not just a facade but a genuine approach to customer outreach and brand revitalization. All in all, Eliason has been able to convince customers on a daily basis that Comcast truly cares and in doing so has set an excellent example of how tweeting can be instrumental to correcting a company's image.

21

American Red Cross
(http://twitter.com/redcross)

YOU MAY BE INTERESTED in Twitter because you want to boost your business or brand, but regardless of whether you plan to use it for profit or not, you also should be aware that the powerful social networking tool is remarkably powerful when it comes to reaching out to and sharing information with your target audience. That said, if your intention is not to sell a product or brand but rather advance the public's awareness of your cause or humanitarian pursuit, I suggest you turn your attention to the manner in which the American Red Cross is leveraging Twitter. The outreach team at the Red Cross has expertly harnessed other social media outlets, like blogs, Facebook, and even Flickr, so it makes sense that the organization has added Twitter to its toolset. After all, in times of need, what better way is there to reach people than with Twitter, thanks to its ability to provide near-immediate information, guidance, and assistance to a nationwide audience? In fact, the tool seems tailor-made for the Red Cross, and the organization has made quick use of Twitter, relying on it to pass along updates, preventative steps, and resources related to almost any disaster, manmade or natural.

Whether a devastating hurricane has just swept through an area, a severe tsunami is fast approaching, or an onslaught of fears and misconceptions about a potential health scare are circulating, the Red Cross effectively uses Twitter to provide instant information to those who need it most. The organization even has mastered the art of embedding compressed URLs in its tweets and utilizes Twitter's linking function to direct followers to sites that provide further important facts, details, and instructions related to the crisis at hand. Beyond information sharing, the Red Cross is also able to send out calls for help and coordinate local volunteerism and donations in disaster locations simply by tweeting. Its mission is certainly not about branding but rather engaging its audience to send aid and information to those in need. And, appropriately enough, the American Red Cross states its social media purpose succinctly:

> The Red Cross belongs to the American people. You fund it, you donate your blood, you prepare for and respond to disasters, you take and instruct first aid classes. You make the Red Cross what it is today, and you hold the keys to its future . . . Social media tools allow us to connect with you on an individual basis at the place where your life intersects with our mission. It makes sense that we would explore these [social media] tools and join these conversations that are an important part of your daily life.

Without a doubt, the American Red Cross demonstrates how maintaining a clear and focused Twitter approach primes an organization to reach and engage people in a meaningful way, whatever their needs may be (see Figure 21-1).

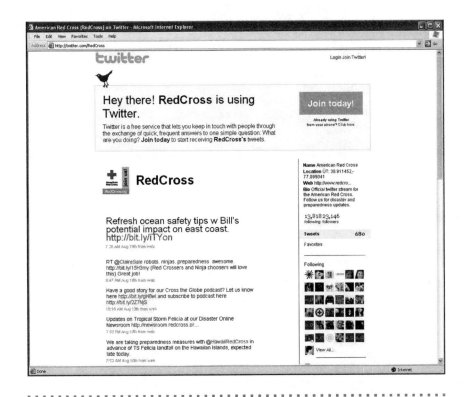

Figure 21-1. The American Red Cross has utilized Twitter to spread timely news, information, and guidance before, during, and after a time of need.

22

Blue Cotton T-Shirts (http://twitter.com/ bluecottontweet)

EVEN THOUGH YOUR CLOSET or armoire might be home to a collection of garments that serve as markers and milestones of your past exploits, none of us ever tires of buying yet another smartly designed T-shirt. Whether we are eager to show off where we went on our summer vacation or are proud to boast our attendance at the year's hottest concert, T-shirts have long enabled us to share our experiences, make a statement, or simply stand in as the billboard for our favorite brands. Sometimes, though, we're at the mercy of those who produce the shirts as to what short-sleeved apparel we can sport over our torsos. And if you have a hobby or interest that is truly niche or nonconformist, you might be hard-pressed to find a shirt that helps you express your passion. That is, you *were* hard-pressed to find the perfect shirt before Blue Cotton launched its operations.

Blue Cotton's entrepreneurial start-up story reads like that of many other young businesses today: a college student, "Mike," was struggling to find post-collegiate employment, so he turned his attention to creating collegiate-themed T-shirts for the students and alumni of Western Kentucky University. Demand blossomed, a website was launched in 2003, and Blue Cotton now employs more than twenty employees. Operating under the tagline "Design what you want," Blue Cotton's online site, http://bluecotton.com, allows customers to easily design their own shirts, hats, and other items of apparel by utilizing the site's handy Flash tools and nearly ten thousand design elements. Whether it's team shirts or corporate-sponsored swag you want to create, Blue Cotton is available 24/7 to help you turn your creative idea into a unique memento.

So how does Twitter fit into Blue Cotton's outreach strategy? Cleverly, the online retailer tweets messages to its customers that include active links to images of their finished products (made possible by the TwitPic Twitter application) when their order is ready to ship. Why is this so clever? Because Blue Cotton's Twitter strategy serves several purposes simultaneously. It allows the company to instantly message customers to let them know that their products are on the way; provide images of the finished products for customers to inspect; and show off to other followers the types of products it can produce. In this way, Blue Cotton showcases its products to customers every day without seeming overly pitch-heavy. After all, the intent of the message was to let the customer know that his order is on the way, right? Further, when Blue Cotton publicly displays its customers' finished products in its tweet stream, the company not only encourages other followers to try their hands at designing something of their own; it also incidentally cross-promotes the customer whose design has been featured, which could even lead to revenue for that customer if and when other followers ask if the newly completed products are for sale.

Blue Cotton has expertly harnessed Twitter to unobtrusively promote its services without pushing for the hard sell. And because the company's products are designed by its customers themselves, Blue Cotton can tweet about its products without offending the social sharing philosophy of Twitter (see Figure 22-1).

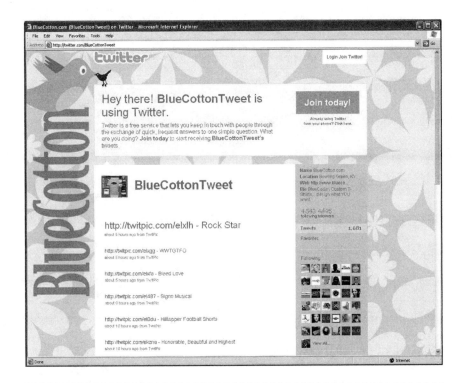

Figure 22-1. Design your own T-shirt at Blue Cotton, and your completed product will be featured in the company's tweet stream when it is on its way to you.

23

Geni (http://twitter.com/geni)

As you begin to spend more and more time on Twitter and other social networking sites, the chances are good that you eventually will see or meet someone who shares your same last name. You smile, consider it a pleasant coincidence, and even possibly use it as an ice-breaker to engage the person in direct conversation. But did you ever ponder whether this individual could be related to you? Some may smirk and dismiss the notion as farfetched, yet the folks behind Geni encourage you to consider the possibility. Cited as one of the Internet's best free-to-use sites in 2008, Geni (http://geni.com) offers its users a social media toolset that enables people to gather together, share messages and photos with one another, and begin to construct their family tree. The site is even able to inform you when one of your relatives first logs in and begins using the Geni toolset, thanks to its ability to detect when one user's information overlaps with another's, and it will subsequently add that individual to your Geni family tree.

Geni adopted Twitter to enrich the soil, so to speak, for those who are actively nurturing their family trees with the social networking site's unique toolset (see Figure 23-1). The tweet stream from Geni provides real-time assistance to users who have questions about the site and its tools or are looking for the best techniques for linking family members together. It also announces new Geni features and tips at the same time that it actively asks followers for feedback on how the site is helping them in their genealogical pursuits. In an effort to add a bit of fun and entertainment to its tweet stream, Geni also tweets about interesting facts and statistics that have been culled from its community members' family trees (nothing private or identifying, of course). Did you know, for example, that the largest Geni tree is now 23 million family members strong?

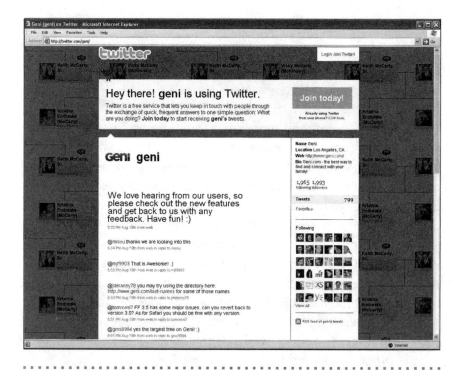

Figure 23-1. Is a big inheritance from an as-yet-unknown relative awaiting you? There could be, and Geni could help you make that connection.

Geni likes to fill its tweet stream with a variety of messages, some of which initiate newcomers to the fun of building a Geni family tree, while others are more informational and include compressed URLs that link to genealogy-related articles and blog postings. And through it all, Geni's tweets maintain a tone on Twitter that is as casual and welcoming as that which drives its family-oriented and downright entertaining social networking site.

24

Ty's Toy Box
(http://twitter.com/tystoybox)

AS A LAST STOP, let's peer into Ty's Toy Box, a relatively new Twitter adopter who, as of this writing, has been tweeting for just a few months but has already gained several hundred followers. Who's Ty, and what's so special about his toy box? In 2003, Ty Simpson formed his company in response to his daughter's desire for character merchandise from her favorite television show at the time, "The Wiggles." To Ty's surprise and eventual disappointment, he discovered that finding character-related toys at his local retail stores was more than a challenge—it was nearly impossible. He responded to his local toy store's shortage of merchandise featuring popular kids' television and movie characters by scouring the world to locate these difficult-to-find licensed products and then reselling them to other parents on http://tystoybox.com. With that, Ty's Toy Box came into being, and in the years since it first was launched, the online retailer has become a hub for folks seeking those hard-to-find items that their kids are clamoring for.

Clearly, Ty is just like any one of us. He is just an average citizen who saw a gap that needed to be filled. He looked left and looked right, and then he looked into the mirror to find the person who would step forward and turn the gap into an opportunity. Ty took to blogging about his business in 2006, sharing updates about new character toys that were in the works, others that would soon be released, and those that were currently available at Ty's Toy Box. He also shared information regarding product licensing, manufacturing, and distribution on his blog, which helped his customers learn more about the items they were purchasing from Ty's Toy Box. In 2009, Ty began tweeting to strengthen his connection with his customers (see Figure 24-1), and since then, he has spent his Twitter time offering his followers links to industry news and announcements while also

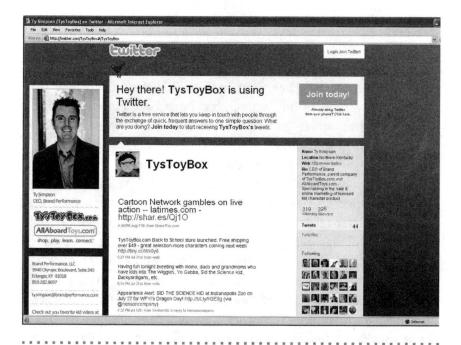

Figure 24-1. When Ty tweets about toys, his smile shines, and his friendliness makes for a pleasant path to profitability.

informing them of sales, coupons, and other special offers. As an added bonus, because Ty stepped into his business almost by accident and is by no means a steely-eyed distributor or reseller, he is able to maintain a friendly tone while he helps others find the toys they're seeking.

Although Ty is still new to tweeting, he is proving that if you approach Twitter with a clear purpose that is grounded in the desire to do good business and forge amiable relationships with others, you can significantly increase and improve your interactions with your customers. Therefore, if you're on the cusp of beginning a business or are ready to increase your company revenues and draw in more clientele, then before you do anything else, turn to Twitter—just ask Ty.

Conclusion: It's Your Turn to Tweet

YOU ARE NOW INFORMED, prepared, and ready to harness Twitter to spread the word about your business or service. In taking up Twitter as a strategic business tool, you are joining the hundreds upon thousands of major brands, labels, companies, and personalities that are adopting the social media site to boost their promotional efforts. You are also doing your clientele a favor in utilizing the social networking tool, in that you are opening up an effective two-way street and fostering a reciprocal relationship with them. Your customers can now tell you what they want, what they need, and what they like—as well as what they *dislike*. Similarly, you can tell them what you have to offer and how you intend to meet their wants and needs, and you can also ask them if you have been successful in serving them.

If Twitter was strictly a one-way medium through which businesses lobbed heavy-handed sales pitches to its customers, the tool likely would tarnish and fade away just as quickly as it gained its current rock-star popularity. However, because it embodies the underlying philosophy of Web 2.0, wherein it is individuals who drive the content-sharing and conversation rather than merely consume it, the future looks bright for Twitter and for businesses that recognize its intrinsic value for both themselves and their customers.

Jack Dorsey and the team at Twitter have put within your grasp an immensely powerful tool that allows you to engage in quick, concise, yet informational interactions with your target audience, and this book has shown you how to harness its power to benefit you and your business. In is important to remember, however, that how you choose to incorporate Twitter into your business outreach efforts is entirely up to you. Although you need to work within the rules and regulations of the social networking tool and site, Twitter gives you the freedom to develop creative new ways of reaching out to your customers and peers. Whether you concoct interactive ways of engaging your followers, perhaps by coordinating scavenger hunts, meet-and-greets, or a similar event, or you find compelling new ways to raise their awareness of your products, brand, or services, now is the time to take advantage of all that Twitter has to offer you.

Come on, now. Get your business into the Twitterverse. Your customers are eagerly awaiting your arrival.

Index

Italic page numbers indicate those pages on which figures appear.

About the Author

Dennis L. Prince is a well-recognized and long-trusted advocate for online entrepreneurs. He continues his tireless efforts to instruct, enlighten, and enable e-commerce enthusiasts and business owners, improving his readers' chances of success every step of the way. His perpetual passion for online marketing along with adherence to good business practices has earned him recognition among many industry analysis companies and publishers including Vendio.com, Auctiva.com, and *Entrepreneur* magazine. He has been a guest on highly rated television shows such as MSNBC's "Countdown with Keith Olbermann" and has been interviewed on TechTV, BBCRadio, and CNet Radio.

Beside his previous books about Internet commerce, his vast editorial contributions to industry stalwarts, including Vendio.com (formerly AuctionWatch.com), Krause Publications, Collector Online, and Auctiva.com, have earned him a well-regarded reputation in his ongoing analysis of the e-commerce industry. He likewise maintains active interaction with his ever-expanding personal network of online enthusiasts, power sellers, and passionate collectors, both online and offline.